Henry Adams and His World

TRANSACTIONS

of the

American Philosophical Society

Held at Philadelphia for Promoting Useful Knowledge

VOLUME 83, Part 4

Henry Adams and His World

David R. Contosta
and
Robert Muccigrosso
Editors

THE AMERICAN PHILOSOPHICAL SOCIETY

Independence Square, Philadelphia

1993

Library of Congress Catalog
Card Number-92-76199.
International Standard Book Number 0-87169-834-X
US ISSN 0065-9746

TABLE OF CONTENTS

CONTRIBUTORS

David R. Contosta is Professor and Chair of the History Department at Chestnut Hill College in Philadelphia. He is the author of *Henry Adams and the American Experiment*. He was also a coordinator of the Henry Adams conference at Brooklyn College on 26 and 27 October 1988.

Robert Muccigrosso is Professor of History at Brooklyn College, CUNY and the author of *American Gothic: The Mind and Art of Ralph Adams Cram*. He was the principal organizer of the Brooklyn College Conference on Henry Adams.

Paul Baker is Chair of the American Civilization Program at New York University. He has written books on Richard Morris Hunt and Stanford White.

Edward Chalfant is a former Professor of English at Hofstra University. He is the author of *Both Sides of the Ocean*, the first of a projected three-volume biography of Henry Adams.

Earl N. Harbert is Professor of English at Northeastern University. He has written *The Force so Much Closer Home: Henry Adams and the Adams Family* and is the editor of Adams's works for *The Library of America*.

Ari Hoogenboom is Professor of History at Brooklyn College, CUNY and the CUNY Graduate Center. A well-known Gilded Age scholar, his most recent studies have concerned the life and presidency of Rutherford B. Hayes.

Eugenia Kaledin is the author of *The Education of Mrs. Henry Adams*.

Alfred Kazin is Distinguished Professor (Emeritus) of English, CUNY Graduate School and University Center. He is known for numerous works in American literary criticism.

John Lukacs is Professor of History at Chestnut Hill College. He is a multi-faceted scholar whose many books deal with various aspects of the European and American past.

Peter Shaw is author of *The Character of John Adams*.

INTRODUCTION

Henry Adams spent much of his adult life trying to make sense of the world around him. This ongoing struggle to grasp the realities of a rapidly changing scene became the focus of his most famous books, as well as a constant refrain in the thousands of letters that he wrote to family, friends, and professional correspondents. Although he often despaired of ever coming to grips with his times, Adams's unbounded curiosity remained unabated to the end of his long life.[1]

In his quest for enlightenment, Adams enjoyed extraordinary advantages. As he felicitously admitted in *The Education of Henry Adams*, "probably no child, born in the year [1838], held better cards than he."[2] Chief among these were his famous name and numerous family connections, for he was no less than the great-grandson of President John Adams and the grandson of President John Quincy Adams. His father, Charles Francis Adams, was a political force in his own right and one of the country's most respected diplomats.[3] Presidents and diplomats were thus as familiar to Henry Adams as aunts, uncles, and grandparents to less

---

[1]The most complete biography of Henry Adams remains the three-volume work by Ernest Samuels: *The Young Henry Adams* (Cambridge, Mass., 1948); *Henry Adams: The Middle Years* (Cambridge, Mass., 1958); and *Henry Adams: The Major Phase* (Cambridge, Mass., 1964). Samuels has also written a one-volume condensation of this trilogy, including new materials that have come to light since the earlier publications: *Henry Adams* (Cambridge, Mass., 1989). The first of a planned, three-volume biography by Edward Chalfant has also appeared: *Both Sides of the Ocean: A Biography of Henry Adams: His First Life, 1838–1862* (Hamden, Conn., 1982). A highly readable one-volume biography is Elizabeth Stevenson's *Henry Adams* (New York, 1956). Among the many monographs on various aspects of Adams's life and works are Max I. Baym, *The French Education of Henry Adams* (New York, 1951); David R. Contosta, *Henry Adams and the American Experiment* (Boston, 1980); Timothy Paul Donovan, *Henry Adams and Brooks Adams* (Norman, Okla., 1961); William Dusinberre, *Henry Adams: The Myth of Failure* (Charlottesville, Va., 1980); William Jordy, *Henry Adams, Scientific Historian* (New Haven, Conn., 1952); and J. C. Levenson, *The Mind and Art of Henry Adams* (Stanford, 1957).

[2]Henry Adams, *The Education of Henry Adams* (Boston, 1918), 4.

[3] On the Adams family, see James Truslow Adams, *The Adams Family* (New York, 1930); Francis Russell, *Adams, An American Dynasty* (New York, 1976); and Jack Shepherd, *The Adams Chronicles* (Boston, 1975). An insightful study of Henry's relationship to his family is Earl N. Harbert, *The Force So Much Closer Home: Henry Adams and the Adams Family* (New York, 1977). On Adams's special relationship to his nieces, see Abigail Adams Homans, *Education by Uncles* (Boston, 1966). For studies of Adams's wife, Marian Hooper "Clover" Adams, see Otto Friedrich, *Clover* (New York, 1979) and Eugenia Kaledin, *The Education of Mrs. Henry Adams* (Philadelphia, 1981).

favored children. When he was twelve Charles Francis Adams took him to Washington where they dropped by the White House as a matter of course for a private talk with President Zachary Taylor. Back in Boston, where the family resided most of the year (with summers spent at the ancestral homestead in nearby Quincy), Senator Charles Sumner was a frequent quest, as well as an intimate friend. Then during Henry's grand tour of Europe (1858–1860), family connections allowed him to meet and interview the Italian revolutionary leader, Giuseppe Garibaldi.

The seven years (1861–1868) that Henry spent in England as a private secretary to his father (who had been appointed the American minister to Great Britain) added dozens of names to his growing list of acquaintances, friends, and international celebrities. Besides being presented at court to Queen Victoria, the young Adams met such political luminaries as Prime Minister Palmerston, reformers John Bright and Richard Cobden, and political philosopher John Stuart Mill. His social world also extended to literary giants such as Robert Browning and Charles Dickens—and to Britain's foremost geologist, Sir Charles Lyell, who had recently embraced Charles Darwin's still hotly contested theory of evolution.[4] It was likewise during his years in Great Britain that Henry made a life-long friend in Charles Milnes Gaskell. Gaskell and his father, James Milnes Gaskell, moved in liberal circles and were well connected politically and socially. Adams and the younger Milnes would share a devotion to political reform in their respective countries and would carry on a fascinating trans-Atlantic correspondence that spanned half a century.

After returning from England Adams continued to maintain creative connections with the prominent and mighty. As a young free-lance journalist in Washington (1868–1870) he enjoyed frequent and direct access to Attorney General William Evarts, Secretary of the Treasury Hugh McCulloch, and Secretary of War John M. Schofield, all superb contacts for a young man bent on making his name as an investigative journalist. In later years, after he had settled permanently in Washington (1877–1918), Adams was a frequent guest at White House dinners and receptions, especially during the administration of his friend Theodore Roosevelt. But by far his most important friend in government

---

[4]The young Adams brashly volunteered to review the tenth edition of Lyell's *Principles of Geology* (1867). The piece appeared in the *North American Review* for October 1868. See Samuels, *Young Henry Adams*, 161–167.

was John Hay, who was secretary of state (1898–1905) during seven of the most momentous years in American history, as the nation rose to great power status. Adams's house on Lafayette Square also became a mecca for artists and writers. William and Henry James, John La Farge, Augustus Saint-Gaudens, Henry Hobson Richardson, and scores of others passed through its portals at one time or another.[5]

During his career as a professional historian (ca. 1870–1890), Adams's far-flung social ties continued to open doors. George Bancroft, renowned American historian and cousin to Adams's wife Marian ("Clover" Hooper) corresponded frequently with Adams, critiqued his manuscripts, and while minister to Germany introduced Adams to a number of notable historians, including Theodor Mommsen and Heinrich von Gneist. Through his personal connections in England, Adams arranged to meet famous British historians such as Sir Henry Maine and William Stubbs. Even James Russell Lowell, one of Adams's professors at Harvard, happened to be the American minister to Spain at the very moment when Henry needed to search the Spanish archives for his massive *History of the United States During the Administrations of Thomas Jefferson and James Madison*.

When Adams traveled for pleasure, he enjoyed the status of a visiting dignitary. The staffs of American legations went out of their way to assist him, and often he was the personal guest of the American minister. While traveling in the South Pacific (1890–1891), he was hailed by native leaders as a great American chief; in Tahiti he was formally adopted by the ruling family. When he went to Mexico in 1896 with his friend, U.S. Senator Donald Cameron, they were met at the railroad station by a military band and then wined and dined by President Porfirio Diaz. When he was not the recipient of such special treatment, Adams still managed to travel in great comfort, a privilege made possible by his substantial inheritance. In the early twentieth century his funds amounted to about $60,000 per year, equivalent to an annual, after-tax income of well over a million dollars in the early 1990s.

This access to the world and its leaders placed Adams in an unparalleled position to observe his contemporaries, and the events

---

[5]On Adams's many friends there are Patricia O'Toole, *The Five of Hearts: An Intimate Portrait of Henry Adams and His Friends* (New York, 1990) and Ernest Scheyer, *Circle of Henry Adams* (Detroit, 1970). Also very helpful in understanding Adams and his rich social connections is Harold Dean Cater's lengthy introduction to his collection of Adams letters, *Henry Adams and His Friends* (Boston, 1947). An exploration of the intimate friendship between Adams and Elizabeth Cameron may be found in Arline B. Tehan, *Henry Adams in Love* (New York, 1983).

that swirled about them. These advantages, combined with his innate curiosity, high native intelligence, insatiable curiosity, and love of criticism made Adams one of the most important writers and thinkers of his age.

In order to commemorate the 150th anniversary of Adams's birth a number of scholars gathered at Brooklyn College on 26 and 27 October 1988 to deliver papers and discuss the life of this famous, and often controversial, man of letters. One likes to think that Adams would have approved of this assembly. Perhaps he would have; perhaps not. Even if he did, his propensity for self-abnegation, honed to a fine point, might preclude any such admission. Or his approval might have come cloaked in so many layers of reservation and waspishness that it would not seem like approval at all. It was just this sort of ambiguity and ambivalence that surrounded the publication of Adams's *Mont-Saint-Michel and Chartres*. After some cajoling, the architect Ralph Adams Cram convinced Adams to allow the American Institute of Architects to publish an edition of this privately printed work. But when the public edition appeared in 1913, Adams complained to Charles Milnes Gaskell about the way in which "the Society of Architects has stolen my volume. . . ." A few weeks later he added to Gaskell, "Don't say I let 'em publish *Chartres*. I kicked so as to be a credit to my years."[6]

This self-deprecating ambivalence is just one of the themes in Adams's multifaceted life that were considered at the Brooklyn College symposium. The following essays consider this wide range of Adams's interests—from politics, foreign affairs, religion, culture, and the philosophy of history; to his rich circle of family and friends.

The work that most strikingly embodies this complexity is Adams's *Education*, a book that still enthralls and, as Edward Chalfant notes, can still confuse readers. Although bearing the subtitle, "An Autobiography," the volume is hardly that, according to Chalfant. For him it is "a pathfinding work in a new literary field, the anti-autobiographical." In "Lies, Silence, and Truth in the Writings of Henry Adams," Chalfant traces the intriguing twists and turns, deceptions and misconceptions, thwarted wishes, and errors of judgment that form the history of the *Education*—from its origins to its public appearance just after the au-

---

[6]Henry Adams to Charles Milnes Gaskell, 19 February 1914 and 13 March 1914, in *The Letters of Henry Adams*, edited by J. C. Levenson et al. (Cambridge, Mass., 1988), 6:635, 641. This edition of Adams's letters is the most complete and is likely to remain the definitive collection.

thor's death. Unaware of these sinuous developments, readers have been unable to separate fact from fiction, a problem that continues to bedevil readers of the *Education* today.

The confused fate of his *Education* might well have annoyed Adams. In any case, the reader soon learns (or thinks that he learns) how Adams failed to make his mark in politics during America's Gilded Age. As the heir to an important political family, Adams bitterly resented his nation's failure to heed what he considered his own right and call to public duty. Despite these disappointments, he remained active in politics as an Independent Republican during the years of Reconstruction and Grantism. As Ari Hoogenboom argues in "Henry Adams and Politics," Adams was not the abject political failure that he later deemed himself—a man "smiling in the ruins." On the contrary, he had been instrumental in forcing the Republicans to nominate a reform-minded presidential aspirant in 1876. With the passage of the Pendleton Act in 1883, one of Adams's favorite political causes—that of civil service reform—also became a reality.

Even so, Adams sometimes misconstrued events and trumpeted his fair share of losing causes. But as David R. Contosta demonstrates in his "Henry Adams and the American Century," Adams correctly foresaw pivotal developments far beyond his death. Through examining events between 1895 and 1918, Adams concluded that Great Britain was a declining power as the American star was rising. He also worried that Russia would undergo a revolution that might destabilize the entire western world. Adams's parallel predictions of a Russo-American rivalry, combined with deep concern that the United States would not react to its new international status with sufficient intelligence and restraint, has led Contosta to call Adams "one of the most profound critics of modern America."

Adams's musings on twentieth-century *Realpolitik* in no way obscured, diminished, or contradicted his passionate interest in religion and particularly in medieval Christianity. In "Religion as Culture: Henry Adams's *Mont-Saint-Michel and Chartres*," Alfred Kazin explores the provenance of this literary pilgrimage and paean to medieval life: from the late nineteenth century's renewed interest in the Middle Ages, the courses that Adams taught at Harvard, and his many visits to the churches and cathedrals of France; to his fascination with the cult of the Virgin. Yet Kazin disagrees with some other Adams scholars that it was a quest for religious faith that attracted Adams to the Middle Ages. Rather, it was the medieval mind, grappling with substantial ideas, that fascinated him. In this sense, Adams hoped to recover time—not eternal time—but a time fashioned and measured by humans who had lived in a refulgent past.

As his interest in the Virgin suggests, Adams vested great importance in women, in his personal life as well as in his writing. There was the suicide of his wife Clover, a tragic, central event in Adams's life, and his intimate friendship with Elizabeth Sherman Cameron. There were many other significant women for Adams according to Eugenia Kaledin, who views her subject as a "gender historian" in "Henry Adams's Anthropological Vision as American Identity." According to Kaledin, Adams was a cultural relativist, atypical in a time of racial supremacists. Identifying with the "powerless and exotic," she argues, Adams wrote sympathetically of women, Native Americans like Pocahontas, Tahitian queens, and Japanese Buddhists. In so doing, he became one of the first American historians to appreciate "the anthropological dimensions in interpreting reality."

Adams may not always have identified with the unconventional and the disenfranchised, but he assuredly did associate with the movers and shakers of the American artistic world. In "Henry Adams and the American Artists: The Two Mansions," Paul Baker writes about Adams's many close friendships and acquaintances among painters and architects who altered the artistic landscape. Besides those already mentioned, these included celebrities like Richard Morris Hunt, William Morris Hunt, Charles Follen McKim, and Stanford White. Adams asked the architect Richardson to design adjoining houses for him and his close friend John Hay, and later chose the sculptor Saint-Gaudens to model the ineffable Adams memorial in Rock Creek Cemetery. Baker also believes that these gifted artists added another dimension to Adams's life. As vital and energetic men in both their public and private lives, they offered an ebullient yea-saying to their more retiring and frequently pessimistic friend.

Besides his many influential friends, the world of Henry Adams encompassed his famous family, whose long ancestral shadows and shared memories enmeshed Adams from his earliest days until his death. No one who has read the *Education* can forget Adams's piquant memories of summers spent with grandfather John Quincy Adams at the family homestead in Quincy, and especially his account of how "Old Man Eloquent" had taken him by the hand one hot morning and led him to school in utter silence. One might conclude that Adams harbored only the most tender thoughts about his grandfather Adams. But according to

Peter Shaw, in "A Dissenting View of John Quincy Adams," the truth was far more complex. Shaw writes that Adams "tweaked the aged John Quincy Adams by the nose" in the *Education*—and elsewhere—viewing his grandfather's life as "a tragic progression from ambition to failure."

Moving away from friends and family, John Lukacs examines Henry Adams as a philosopher of history. As Lukacs points out in "Henry Adams and the European Tradition of the Philosophy of History," Adams all but abandoned the writing of history after 1890 for the philosophy of this emerging discipline. Unfortunately, according to Lukacs, Adams embraced a scientism that proved his "undoing" and went on to fashion a philosophy of history that was ultimately "worthless."

Adams may have failed at creating a philosophy of history, but his own insistence on personal failure in the *Education* and elsewhere should not be taken at face value. Here one should follow the admonition of D. H. Lawrence—to trust the tale and not its teller. Earl N. Harbert, for one, sides with Lawrence in his "Failure or Success? Our Legacy from Henry Adams." Despite the discovery of new information on Adams, Harbert believes that we still risk oversimplification in trying to assess Adams's rightful place as a writer and historian. Given his continuing influence, especially as a historian, Harbert concludes that Adams's life was largely successful.

To gauge Adams's work from a somewhat different perspective: Stendhal defined a classic as a work that continued to find readers a century after it was written. By this criterion several of Adams's works are already classics, with others nearly so. What the future may hold for Adams's reputation, no one can say—save that his bicentenary should prove very enlightening.

David R. Contosta
Chestnut Hill College
Philadelphia, Pennsylvania

Robert Muccigrosso
Brooklyn College of the City
University of New York

LIES, SILENCE, AND TRUTH IN THE WRITINGS OF HENRY ADAMS

Edward Chalfant

In February 1907, Henry Adams began to distribute copies of a work he had privately printed. The copies were large and had wide margins. To use terms Adams used, the pages were "sheets" or "proof-sheets."[1] The copies were not strictly books. They were devices to permit further work on a book. The margins were wide to facilitate the writing of corrections and improvements in the form expected by printers.

On receiving a copy in 1907, each recipient found on its binding a label saying only

The
Education
of
Henry
Adams

Inside, the recipient found a title page saying only

The Education
of
Henry Adams

———

Washington
1907

Here is one of Adams's silences. As privately printed, his *Education* avoided naming its author.

The avoidance belonged to a pattern. Adams privately printed two versions of his *Mont-Saint-Michel and Chartres*, in 1904 and 1912. By his order, each version began with a title page like the

---

[1]See especially HA to Henry Lee Higginson, 1 Apr 1907, in J. C. Levenson et al., editors, *The Letters of Henry Adams* (Cambridge, Mass. and London, 1988) (hereafter *Letters*), 6: 58: "The volume—or rather, the sheets of the possible projected book. . . ."

title page of his *Education;* neither named the author. Similarly, in 1911, when Henry Cabot Lodge and his wife were about to publish a small book Adams had written at their request about their son George Cabot Lodge, Adams wrote to Elizabeth Cameron: "If they will only let me keep my name off it!"[2] But the coin had another side. In 1889–1891, Adams acceded to, or required, the printing of his name on the title pages of his *History of the United States* and its companion volume, his *Historical Essays.* And in 1910, privately printing *A Letter to American Teachers of History,* he directed the printer to compose a title page that said

by
Henry Adams

This phenomenon—Adams's keeping his name off some title pages and permitting its appearance on other title pages—was presumably meaningful. I suggest that we seek its meaning by studying his behavior in one instance, as author of *The Education of Henry Adams.* He sent a copy to Clara Hay. She looked at it and wrote him a letter saying he should read the Bible.[3] He did not need the admonition; he had read the Bible. But, fortunately for us, her letter elicited a reply by Adams containing the following statements:

All my life I have tried to ignore self and selfishness either in this world or the next. . . .

All I have sought has been the direction, or tendency, or history, of the human mind, not as religion or science, but as fact,—as a whole, or stream,—and this with no view to its relation to me or my benefit.[4]

These statements, I believe, go a long way to explain why Adams saw to it that *The Education of Henry Adams,* when privately printed, did not name an author. I think the statements go a long way to explain why Adams in every phase of life produced anonymous and pseudonymous works. Also, in my opinion, they can help us realize that Adams sometimes resorted to silence as a means of strong expression. We can say that he twice powerfully declared an intention to "ignore self," once in strong words in a

---

[2]HA to Elizabeth Cameron, 7 Feb 1911, *Letters* 6: 412.
[3]Clara Hay to HA, 6 May 1907, HA Papers, Massachusetts Historical Society (hereafter MHS).
[4]HA to Clara Hay, 15 May 1907, *Letters,* 6: 67–68.

letter to Clara Hay, once in extremely assertive silence on the label and title page of his greatest work.

As privately printed, *The Education of Henry Adams* had no table of contents. The reader proceeded directly from the title page to a two-page preface. At the bottom of its first page, the preface exhibited a striking phrase, "a monument of warning against the *Ego.*" "*Ego*" was a term Adams used interchangeably with "self."

An early recipient of *The Education*, perhaps the earliest, was Henry's elder brother Charles. Evidence abounds that Charles Francis Adams, Jr., was an inveterate egoist. Where Henry's passions included ignoring self, Charles's passions began with remembrance of self. In secret, Charles had gone to work as an autobiographer. He had written three manuscript volumes of *Memorabilia* and had made some efforts to prepare an "autobiographical sketch."[5]

On receiving Henry's *Education*, Charles read chapter 1. Things he could have noticed were that the text is a narrative; it begins with the birth of a child; it tells the child's story in the third person; and it consistently refers to the child when grown as "Henry Adams." What Charles did notice is clear in his own words. He wrote to Henry expressing delight but also puzzlement: ". . . the first chapter . . . is charming . . . to me uniquely delightful. Why didn't you let out your own most vivid recollections . . . ?" In part, the elder brother recognized *The Education* as charming recollections; hence good autobiography. In part, he read it as incomplete, less-vivid recollections; hence second-best autobiography.[6]

I am not derogating Charles's first reaction. *The Education of Henry Adams* was something unexpected in the way of books. No one could fairly be asked to guess its drift after one reading of its opening chapter. Today, after innumerable complete readings by a great many persons, Henry's amazing narrative continues to elude positive characterization. Trying to form a comprehensive understanding of the book, wise readers may begin by venturing merely negative and partial comments. In this instance, Henry was not an autobiographer. His *Education* is not an autobiography. If it is in some percentage or fraction an autobiography, the mite is so small as not to warrant the description. The genius of the book

---

[5]The *Memorabilia* are in the CFA2 Papers, MHS. For "autobiographical sketch," see note by W. C. F. [Worthington Chauncey Ford] following the title page of *Charles Francis Adams/ 1835–1915/ An Autobiography* (Boston and New York, 1916) (hereafter *Autobiography*). Internal evidence suggests that CFA2 began work on the sketch in 1900. See 54 (in contrast with 56) and 83.

[6]Worthington Chauncey Ford, ed., *Letters of Henry Adams/ 1892–1918* (Boston and New York, 1938), 2: 47 2n.

can perhaps be found in its being—among other things—a path-finding work in a new literary field, the anti-autobiographical. For just these reasons, strange things were bound to happen in the early 1900s when copies were read by persons who themselves, in practice or at heart, were autobiographers.

On 17 February 1908, Worthington Chauncey Ford wrote to Adams asking for a copy of a book by him called *My Influences*. Adams replied that he was not sure what book Ford was referring to. Writing a second time, Ford explained: "The particular book I had in mind I have heard of as an 'autobiography' or as 'My Influences'—meaning the influences under which you fell at different periods of your life."[7] Adams was far from eager to give copies of *The Education* merely because a copy was requested. He sometimes lent copies, and there were cases in which lent copies were returned to him. As it happened, he gave a copy to Ford, and with good reason.[8] Ford's letters had permitted him to see which way the wind was blowing. Rumors were circulating that he had written and printed an autobiography; that the book was written in the first person; and that the words on its title page were something on the order of

> *My Influences*
> *An Autobiography*
>
> by
> Henry Adams

Needless to say, once people heard of a new privately printed book by Adams that was an autobiography, they knew it was a factual account of his experiences, providing data about his intimates, beginning, or ending, with his wife. On inspection, however, the book was found to offer only a broken narrative which effectively stopped in 1871, months before Henry Adams and Clover Hooper were engaged, and resumed in 1892, six years after Mrs. Adams died. Accordingly *The Education of Henry Adams* speedily acquired a reputation as the great American autobiography in which the author leaves out his wife.

Readers considerate enough to return a borrowed copy were Fred and Blanche Tams. On 3 April 1908, Adams told Mrs. Tams

---

[7] Ford to HA, 17 Feb and 19 Feb 1908, HA Papers, MHS.

[8] Ford's copy is at the Houghton Library, Harvard University. It contains (among other things) transcriptions by Ford of most of the annotations to be found in the so-called Thayer copy. See notes 10 and 11.

in a letter what, mainly, he left out of the narrative. Lest his meaning be missed, I shall put it in my words, then quote his. In my words, two things were excluded: Henry Adams and autobiography. Admittedly the narrative has a protagonist—a particular self or ego. Admittedly the protagonist is given the name "Henry Adams" and his adventures at first sight may appear to be factual throughout; but, speaking of the narrative, Adams said to Mrs. Tams: ". . . try . . . to think of it as what it was written for—a serious effort to reform American education by showing what it ought to be. The Ego is a purely imaginary fiction."[9]

If we take Adams at his word, the silence in *The Education* is huge, the ignoring of self is huge, and a lie is huge. Saying to Mrs. Tams that the ego in his book is "a purely imaginary fiction," Adams told her that the Henry Adams who figures as the protagonist is a total lie; or, if the phrase seems not quite accurate, the completest possible lie consistent with the narrative's being read and liked.

I realize that extreme statements may appear to be creeping into this paper. I realize as well that Adams has a reputation for dealing in hyperbole, and frankly I would prefer not to share it. So I suggest we court the safety of some small silences and lesser lies. I would prefer, too, that we break this narrative and jump to 1914.

In Washington, in January 1914, Adams lent a copy of his *Education* to William Roscoe Thayer, to help him complete a biography of John Hay. Thayer lived in Massachusetts and was corresponding secretary of the Massachusetts Historical Society. At some point, he learned that the copy lent to him by Adams contained scores of annotations in Adams's handwriting. Most, but not all, had the form of instructions to the printer, should the book again be set in type.[10]

I have been investigating the history of the copy Adams lent to Thayer. My present opinion of its history includes the following propositions:

—in Washington, while lending the copy of Thayer, Adams was silent about its containing annotations;
—after learning that the copy contained annotations, Thayer was silent—he did not tell Adams that the copy contained annotations;

---

[9]HA to Blanche Tams, 3 Apr 1908, and HA to James Frederic Tams, 7 Apr 1908, *Letters*, 6: 130–132.

[10]The copy is owned by the Massachusetts Historical Society. Thayer wrote on the flyleaf in ink, "Wm. R. Thayer/ Washington/ January 1914." Scholarly authorities (see items b through e in note 11) first asserted, apparently on the basis of this inscription, that HA *gave* Thayer the copy. Subsequently, and more prudently, they have asserted that HA *lent* it (see item f in note 11).

—Thayer believed the copy to be a literary property of great importance;
—he resolved to keep the copy as long as possible, preferably until after Adams died;
—he let two persons into his secret: Worthington Ford, who in 1909 became editor of publications at the Massachusetts Historical Society, and Ferris Greenslet, an editor at Houghton Mifflin Company, the Boston firm that would publish the biography of John Hay.[11]

You may sense that the plot is thickening, and it is. The story of *The Education of Henry Adams* was never simple and in its later stages, after 1908, became increasingly complicated.

A year later, Lindsay Swift, the librarian of the Boston Public Library, asked Charles Francis Adams, Jr., to urge his brother Henry to give the library a copy of *The Education*. Charles wrote to Henry as desired. On 20 January 1915, Henry replied: "Will you kindly convey to Mr[.] Swift my regrets that I can't gratify his wish. The sheets of the Education were sent out near ten years ago for correction and suggestion. . . . None remain to distribute."[12] The statement "None remain to distribute" must be read with caution. If Henry meant he had no copies of *The Education* in his Washington house, the statement was false. But at some point after getting the edition from the printer, Henry had divided the

---

[11]The propositions, I believe, are explicit and/or implicit in the chief published writings about the Thayer copy. The propositions seem reasonable but should be accepted only conditionally. The history of HA's correction and improvement of *The Education* has been investigated fitfully and in haste, without attention to much evidence already available, not to speak of other evidence that should be searched for.

The chief writings about the Thayer copy are listed below. In fairness, the items should be read together and in chronological order. The first three items are very seriously weakened by an error of dating by Cater (item a), which Samuels and Munford repeat (b, c), and Samuels discovers (d), with the result that the writers thereafter are at pains to counteract it (d, e, f).

a. *Henry Adams and His Friends/ A Collection of His Unpublished Letters*, compiled with a biographical introduction by Harold Dean Cater (Boston, 1947), lxxxviii-xci, 769–770 (hereafter Cater).

b. Ernest Samuels, *Henry Adams/ The Major Phase* (Cambridge, Mass., 1964), 559–571, 658.

c. Howard N. Munford, "Thayer, Ford, Goodspeed's, and Middlebury: a Missing Copy of *The Education of Henry Adams* Found," MHS *Proceedings*, 83–84 (1971): 148–153.

d. Howard N. Munford, "A Third Annotated Copy of *The Education of Henry Adams*," MHS *Proceedings*, 85 (1973): 107–114.

e. [Henry Adams], *The Education of Henry Adams*, edited with an introduction and notes by Ernest Samuels/ Jayne N. Samuels, assistant editor, Boston 1974, textual note, appendix B.

f. Henry Adams, *Novels/ Mont Saint Michel/ The Education*, New York (Library of America) 1983, 1219–1225. (All material in this volume relating to *The Education* was prepared by the Samuelses. See the prefatory acknowledgment.)

[12]CFA2 Papers, MHS. The letter includes a statement: "As a member of the Hist. Soc.ʸ I did, however, give a copy to your [the MHS] Library, the only copy, I think, accessible to the public." The copy thus given by HA to MHS for its library is not currently in evidence.

copies into groups, one group for distribution, the other for his own use. What he said in January 1915 thus was possibly true in the sense that he no longer had distribution copies. They were gone.

Two months later, on 20 March 1915, Charles died. Henry always loved Charles, and the elder brother's death had almost inestimable meaning for the younger. But also the elder's death had unparalleled meaning for the Massachusetts Historical Society. It was the custom of the society, when a member died, to honor him by preparing, hearing, and printing a biographical memoir. In the case of Charles Adams, no ordinary memoir would serve. He had been president of the society for twenty years. He had practically refounded the society, had housed its staff and its holdings in a new building, and had even solved the problem of an exceptional memoir. In 1912–1913, partly in an effort to match his brother Henry's *Education* as he understood it, he had completed his "autobiographical sketch," placed the manuscript in a sealed package, given it to the society, and authorized Ford as editor to publish it at the appropriate time.[13]

The member chosen as the society's new president was Henry Cabot Lodge.[14] Over the years, Lodge had come under the influence of Charles Adams, whom he admired. Like Charles, Lodge was self-important. In 1913, he had published *Early Memories*, the first volume of what he hoped in time might become a two-volume autobiography.[15]

During the remaining months of 1915, Lodge and Ford worked energetically to memorialize the society's deceased president. Their plans called for a public meeting of the society and the publication of a full-sized book. The meeting would take place in the First Church in Boston and would feature an address by Lodge. The book, to be published by Houghton Mifflin Company, would contain the deceased president's "autobiographical sketch." On backstrip and title page, the copies would bear the words

Charles Francis Adams
1835–1915
An Autobiography

---

[13]HA evidently knew a certain amount about CFA2's autobiographical efforts, and he positively suggested that CFA2 complete an account of himself. See HA to CFA2, 10 Nov 1911, *Letters*, 6: 480: ". . . we had better do our own epitaphs, and do them quick."

For the date CFA2 completed the sketch, see *Autobiography*, 211; and for data concerning the package, use of the sketch, etc., see ibid., Ford's prefatory note.

[14]CFA2 suggested the election of Lodge as his successor. See Ford to CFA2, 3 Mar 1913, CFA2 Papers, MHS.

[15]For his desire to add a volume, see Lodge to Ford, 15 Mar 1923, Lodge Papers, MHS.

Since the sketch Charles supplied would fill only slightly more than two hundred pages, there was space for more material. Ford wrote a prefatory note and an extension of the narrative, carrying it forward to the author's death. Lodge's address would serve as the introduction.

When preparations for the meeting and the publication of the book were far advanced, on 28 September 1915, Mrs. Lodge died. Her death affected the way her widower could behave with respect to Henry Adams. Mrs. Lodge and Henry Adams had been close friends. She would have frowned on any liberties taken in his connection.[16]

In the First Church on 15 November, Lodge delivered an address in which, while saying how highly he thought of Charles Adams, he said—without stating who was meant—how much he had been graveled by Henry Adams. Lodge's complaints against Henry were substantially the same as Charles's complaints.[17] Near the end of the address, Lodge included a passage which can be reduced by ellipsis to the following:

We have had of late . . . a school . . . of paradox makers. . . . A paradox is merely an inverted platitude or truism. . . . If a man stands on his head in the street, he is sure to attract momentary attention. . . . With . . . paradox . . . Charles Adams had no relation whatever. . . . He . . . did not . . . hold up with factitious admiration some long dead century, or some foreign country as an ideal where all was perfect. . . . He was not a pessimist, and professional pessimism had, for him, no attraction.[18]

You will not be surprised if I say that the passage was intended to be recognized when heard in Boston as sharply critical of Henry Adams and three of his books: *Mont-Saint-Michel and Chartres, The*

---

[16]How HA related to Lodge and Mrs. Lodge is vivid in a passage, HA to Elizabeth Cameron, 16 Jul 1905, *Letters*, 6: 693: "Sister Anne [Mrs. Lodge] wanted me to go to Chartres with them on Friday. As it happened, I was not in a state to go, but in any case I cannot venture myself any longer with Cabot. He has become physically repulsive to me. It is very hard. Of course one is perfectly transparent. She [Mrs. Lodge] sees every shade of my feelings. We keep up a sort of mask-play together, each knowing the other to the ground. She kept it up with Hay to the end. It has gone on for years, and may go for more, but only on condition that I do not let my irritability show itself."

[17]CFA2 expressed his complaints against HA in a letter to their sister Mary, 29 Jan 1913, CFA2 Paper, MHS: ". . . he [HA] has fallen back completely into his old Washington ways. We . . . see but little of him. He never comes to the house [CFA2's Washington house at 1701 Massachusetts Avenue], confining his society largely to his coterie of females. With them he is as fantastic as of yore, indulging in boundless paradox and in efforts at conversational and other affectations and eccentricities, of which my more sober and possibly a bit critical judgment, fails wholly to approve. The coterie in his case, as in that of lamented Bunthorne [a parody of Oscar Wilde in Gilbert and Sullivan's *Patience*], sit around looking at him with admiring eyes, and say:—'Oh, how delightful he is!' "

[18]*Autobiography*, lv-lvi.

Education of Henry Adams, and *A Letter to American Teachers of History.* And you will not be surprised to hear that Adams was not present in the church.

What is surprising is that Lodge shortly supplied complete proofs of the address to Henry Adams in Washington. Adams read them and responded with a letter of unconditional praise. He said: "A thousand thanks! You have done it with a good feeling, a thoroughness, a conscientiousness, and an appreciation that puts us all at your feet."[19]

Soon after, on behalf of Houghton Mifflin, Ferris Greenslet wrote to Adams asserting that he, Adams, was rumored to be considering public issuance of *The Education.* Greenslet asked: "May we . . . have the privilege of issuing your autobiographic book? It would be a . . . pleasure to us if, following the publication next spring of the *Autobiography of Charles Francis Adams. . . ,* we could announce the publication in the autumn of *The Education of Henry Adams.*"[20]

Greenslet's letter was one of several pressures which, in February 1916, led Adams to look for a certain copy of *The Education* in his Washington house. This action, in turn, led him to write to Charles Milnes Gaskell, an English friend:

. . . you remember my "Education." Publishers have been worrying me to let them publish it. . . . Of course I refused, but in doing so I looked for the copy I had corrected for that purpose near ten years ago. To my great annoyance, it had disappeared. . . . Apparently some one—probably myself—has made free with my literary remains, for books are missing out of sets.[21]

Attempting to deal with this passage, scholars interested in Adams have held that there was one fully-corrected copy of *The Education;* that Adams annotated the copy a "few years later" than 1908 but "prior to 1912"; that he lent it to Thayer in 1914; that in 1916, looking for the copy in his Washington house, Adams did not find it and thought it had "disappeared" when really all that happened was that he suffered a memory lapse—forgot he had lent it to Thayer; and, further, when writing to Gaskell, Adams forgot he had corrected the copy only five to seven years previously, as opposed to his stated "near ten."[22]

---

[19]HA to Lodge, Thursday [18? Nov 1915], *Letters,* 6: 705.
[20]HA Papers, MHS.
[21]HA to Gaskell, 18 Mar 1916, *Letters,* 6: 726.
[22]See items c through f in note 11, above.

I want to suggest that it may be risky, as well as demeaning, to attribute memory lapses to Henry Adams concerning his own books and dates in his own life. I think it possible that Adams in 1916 remembered that he lent an annotated copy of *The Education* to Thayer in 1914. I can believe that the copy thought by Thayer to be important was in Adams's view comparatively unimportant—so much so that he had relegated it to lesser uses, such as assistance to Thayer. I would give serious heed to the hypothesis that Adams on that fateful day was looking for a different copy of *The Education;* that in some undisclosed sense it did disappear; and that he had in a measure corrected it for publication in 1906–1907. In short, I can imagine that Adams, writing the quoted passage to Gaskell, may have written not one syllable or mark that was untrue.[23]

Subsequent to the shock of not finding a certain copy of his *Education*, Adams began a sequence of actions which is in process of reconstruction. Drawing on copies of *The Education* he had reserved for his own use, Adams slightly corrected one of the copies. In addition, he wrote an "Editor's Preface." He then made an arrangement with Lodge, permitting him to publish *The Education* posthumously on condition that it appear precisely as he, Adams, had modified it in that one copy; also on condition that it include the editor's preface, signed by Lodge. At his house on 1 March 1916, Adams signed the editor's preface with Lodge's initials, inserted the added preface in the slightly corrected copy, and sent the copy to Lodge in a sealed package.[24] In turn, Lodge mailed the package to Ford at the Massachusetts Historical Society.

---

[23]At the end of item d in note 11, above, Munford says: "One is tempted to conclude that all the annotated and corrected copies of the *Education* are accounted for, but we cannot be certain." While commendably cautious, the remark oddly is offered with reference to the copy HA said he gave to MHS for its library. (HA's statement about the copy does *not* suggest he annotated or corrected it. See note 12, above.)

I am suggesting caution in relation to something different and possibly important: the copy HA said in 1916 he had found to have "disappeared." According to HA, the copy was "corrected" in 1906–1907 and to the best of his knowledge in February 1916 should have been at a certain place in his Washington house. There is nothing intrinsically incredible in the description. The description fits neither the Thayer copy nor a similarly annotated copy once held by the Boston Athenaeum. (I presently own the latter and urge its being called the Paris copy, since it once belonged to HA's Paris library.) If the description applies to any copy, it is to one not yet discussed in the literature.

Who is to say that a copy corresponding to HA's description (a) did not exist and (b) will not be found?

[24]Initially verbal, HA's agreement with Lodge took written form in the covering letter, HA to Lodge, 1 Mar 1916, *Letters*, 6: 725: ". . . I wish that you [Lodge], on behalf of the Hist. Society, would take charge of the matter, and see that the volume is printed as I leave it." The slightly corrected copy, known as the Abernethy copy, is owned by Middlebury College. Many details concerning it may be found in items c through f in note 11, above.

Two weeks later, on 15 March 1916, drawing again on copies he had reserved for his own use, Adams sent a wholly uncorrected copy of *The Education*, with instructions, to George Lathrop Rives, a lawyer and historian in New York. In keeping with the instructions, the copy was placed in the Reserve Division of the New York Public Library. After Adams's death, it was quietly catalogued and given a call number. It remains in superb condition and has been little noticed.[25] Why Adams placed the copy in that library in that way is not clear. His actions were in part mysterious.

More must be said about the "Editor's Preface" that Adams inserted in the slightly corrected copy he sent to Lodge. In *The Education of Henry Adams* when published, the editor's preface would precede the preface itself, the two-page affair that had always been a feature of the book. Thus the book, as changed by Adams in 1916, would begin with an editor's sentence:

This volume, written in 1905 as a sequel to the same author's "Mont-Saint-Michel and Chartres," was privately printed, to the number of one hundred copies, in 1906, and sent to the persons interested, for their assent, correction, or suggestion.

I hope you will excuse me if I say that in one respect (and possibly others) the sentence may be a lie; for it was later alleged—and may be true—that the copies totaled only forty. If forty was the true number and he remained aware of the fact when he wrote the editor's preface, Henry Adams insured that his greatest book when published would start with a sentence signed by Henry Cabot Lodge which to the extent of including a wrong number would be deceiving.[26]

---

[25]The Reserve Division is now the Rare Book Division. The copy contains a slip, pasted inside the cover, on which is written in ink: " 'The Education of Henry Adams'/ Sent to G. L. R. 25 March 1916/ for the N. Y. Public Library/ Not to be put in the library catalogue until after the author's death and not [to be] put into circulation." A penciled note, also pasted inside the cover, adds, "This ink note [is] in the handwriting of George L. Rives/ hml." The initials "hml" are those of Harry M. Lydenberg, for many years director of the New York Public Library. The copy is stamped RESERVE on the end paper. I am advised by the division's curators that the call mark was put into the copy when it was catalogued in 1918.

The copy's significance is undetermined. Possibly HA wished to assure the survival of at least one copy of the privately-printed sheets in a wholly uncorrected state, knew that the New York Public Library had a Reserve Division whose books did not circulate, and preferred that division as owner of such a copy for that reason.

[26]The earliest HA bibliography is a rare pamphlet, *Bibliography of the Writings of Henry Adams*, compiled by James Truslow Adams, New York (Albert and Charles Boni) 1930. It lists (11): "1907 *The Education of Henry Adams*, privately printed, Washington, 1907, vi, 453pp."

Expanded and revised, the bibliography reappears at the back of James Truslow Adams, *Henry Adams*, New York 1933. The expansions and revisions show considerable biblio-

Adams died on 27 March 1918, in the early morning. That afternoon, Lodge secretly wrote to Ford directing that arrangements to publish *The Education* be made at once. Lodge said, "You remember, of course, that he left to the Society his privately printed 'Education of Henry Adams', which is his autobiography, to be published by the Society as that of his brother Charles was published."[27] In further letters to Ford, not content with describing *The Education* as "his Autobiography," and "the Autobiography," Lodge retitled the book altogether as "The Autobiography of Henry Adams."[28]

Ford did not share Lodge's impulse to substitute a new main title. Instead Ford noticed that the book's title page was incomplete. On 2 May 1918, he wrote to Lodge:

The title page raises a point; to say merely "The Education of Henry Adams" and stop there, gives no indication of authorship, but if the two words "an autobiography" be added, that will be serviceable to those who see the book and to catalogers, and we have to make some concession to the mechanical part of our libraries. Will there be any objection to that form?[29]

---

graphical sophistication. The 1907 entry is changed to read: "*The Education of Henry Adams,* privately printed (40 copies only), Washington, 1907, vi, 453 pp."

The assertion in the revised 1933 bibliography that there were forty copies only was presumably made in full knowledge that the editor's preface at the front of *The Education* as published in 1918 states that there were one hundred copies. If it indeed was made with such knowledge, the 1933 assertion does not simply state the size of an edition; it contradicts a previous statement of the size of an edition. So the assertion is no slight matter.

In item a in note 11 above, Cater states, 591n: "*The Education of Henry Adams*...seems to have first appeared in February of . . . [1907]. At first he [HA] had only forty copies printed, but the demand for it became so great that he had to have more copies made later." Cater cites no evidence that HA had more copies printed, subsequent to an original forty. His statement has the appearance of a gratuitous conflation of irreconcilable sources: the first sentence of HA's "Editor's Preface" and James Truslow Adams's 1907 bibliography entry as revised in 1933.

In b, e, & f, Ernest and Jayne Samuels ring changes on Cater's unsupported statement. See b, 332: ". . . the original forty copies of the privately printed edition—later augmented to one hundred. . . ." Also e, 539: "Forty copies were originally printed. . . . Sixty additional copies were subsequently printed to meet the demand for copies from his friends." And f, 1219: "*The Education of Henry Adams* was printed by Furst and Company in a private edition of forty copies, which was soon increased to one hundred."

Conceivably the number of copies privately printed was higher than forty, but I am reminded of a line in Boswell's *Life of Johnson* (14 Jul 1763): "Let us count our spoons." In that spirit, I have undertaken a census of copies. The census is well along but hardly completed. I have firm knowledge of the whereabouts of twenty-one copies; printed records indicating the fairly recent whereabouts of nine other copies, handwritten and/or verbal attestations of the whereabouts of two additional copies; and a reasonable conjecture as to the destruction of one copy. The total so far is thirty-three copies. I expect the total to grow, but to date I see no chance of its remotely approaching one hundred copies.

[27]Lodge Papers, MHS.

[28]Letters, Lodge to Ford, 4, 6, 8 Apr 1918, Lodge Papers, MHS.

[29]Lodge Papers, MHS.

Lodge had been pledged not to change the book. All the same, he made no objection, and the title page was changed to read

The Education
of Henry Adams

An Autobiography[30]

When the book was ready for sale, Houghton Mifflin was faced with the usual problem of getting large orders. The firm wished to describe the book to bookstores in such terms as would induce them to stock it heavily, well ahead of the Christmas rush. The problem was complicated by a regrettable difficulty. There was something not right about the book. Its main title was ill-chosen—a clear mistake.

Every month, the company sent a circular, *The Piper*, to bookstores and jobbers. The issue of *The Piper* for October 1918 began with "An Announcement *Extraordinary*." The announcement ran to seven paragraphs, including the following:

Fifteen years ago, [Henry Adams] . . . began the composition of the Autobiography which he has quaintly titled "The Education of Henry Adams." He tells the whole story in the third person, as if Henry Adams were not himself, but a hero of fiction, or a subject of a biography by another. He tells it, however, with a vividness and freshness of detail which makes the book as fascinating to read as any novel.

If I may paraphrase, here is the publisher's solution: the title, *The Education of Henry Adams*, is quaint and the person responsible for the quaintness was Adams; however, the book (we all know) is his autobiography; by means of an unusual device, use of the third person, it cleverly sustains an air of being almost fiction; but, be assured, it vividly and freshly sets forth the facts;

---

[30]It has been supposed that the intrusion of the subtitle was the work of the publisher. See item b in note 11 above, 569: "Presumably it was Greenslet who was responsible for adopting the subtitle 'An Autobiography.' " Also see f, xvii: "The focus of the book was somewhat blurred by the subtitle 'An Autobiography' which was added by the publisher."

The full availability of the Lodge Papers has put an end to doubt. While it might still be argued that Greenslet had a voice in the preparation of Ford's letter to Lodge suggesting that "An Autobiography" could be intruded, there is no escape from the revealed, plain evidence that responsibility for the change rests primarily on Lodge, who, as chief editor of the book, approved the intrusion; secondarily on Ford, who suggested the intrusion, giving reasons which perhaps were entirely his own; and tertiarily, if at all, on Greenslet and Houghton Mifflin Company, to whom Ford supplied the title page as changed.

To his credit, Cater stated the main part of this conclusion in 1947. See Cater, xci.

it tells the whole story; and you can bet your bookstore it's going to sell.[31]

In this way, during the twelve years 1907–1918, the stage was set for the coming together of two large-scale lies. Adams gave his *Education* the form of a narrative whose protagonist, called "Henry Adams," was as much a lie as possible—"a purely imaginary fiction." If the book had been published as its author wanted it published, readers in increasing numbers would have seen that the lie was a lie; that sheer fiction was sheer fiction. I can say this for a reason you may have anticipated. There were two Henry Adamses in *The Education of Henry Adams*. One was the imaginable protagonist whose adventures were told in the narrative. The other was the audible Adams in whose unmistakable voice the narrative was told. The two were so dissimilar that the fictitious character of the protagonist was one of the book's most evident, most intriguing features. What was perhaps even more important, the fiction was entirely defensible—defensible because transparent.

The book was not published as Adams wanted it published. Beginning in October 1918, the subtitle "An Autobiography" was successfully sold as an integral part of the book. In advertisements seen by the public, on cover and jacket, and within the book, the subtitle was silently passed off as the author's phrase, as his election, as his meaning. The lie was atrocious—atrocious because opaque. Reviewers, critics, and scholars were given not the slightest hint that the subtitle was an intrusion, still less that it misrepresented and inverted the book. Retail buyers and general readers were effectually assured that the subtitle was supplied by the Adams who tells the narrative. All comers were systematically guided, assisted, and hurried toward misreading.

The consequence was literary disaster. In proportion as they took the subtitle to be Adams's, readers lost the protection the author had given them against mistaking imaginative fiction for simple fact. Reading *The Education of Henry Adams* could have been a salutary experience—one of keeping company with a superbly capable author who can surprise the reader with pointed

---

[31]Anxiety to make the publication profitable was not restricted to Houghton Mifflin Company. The same anxiety was felt by Lodge, who well understood that increased royalties from sales would greatly help the Massachusetts Historical Society as payee. Accordingly he pressed Ford to lose no time. See Lodge to Ford, 27 Mar 1918, Lodge Papers, MHS: "I need not say to you that it [*The Education*] is a very remarkable book, and I think a very great autobiography and will command a large sale. . . . I should think that the sooner we get it ready for the press the better."

silences and ingenious lies that encourage learning and conduce
to truth. Sad to say, the combined reactions of Charles Adams,
Lodge, Ford, Greenslet, and Houghton Mifflin Company turned
the reading of *The Education* into a confused, chaotic experience
good for no one and hurtful to Henry Adams. It is against that
confusion and chaos, I believe, that persons interested in Henry
Adams are still struggling today. I have to say it: confusion is very
far from having ended.

HENRY ADAMS AND POLITICS

ARI HOOGENBOOM

Henry Adams was born to politics. His political ambitions for himself, his family, and his associates, whom we call reformers or Independents (who advocated the gold standard, free trade, and civil service reform), dominated his life from 1860 to 1876. His reactions to political leaders, like William Henry Seward, Abraham Lincoln, Charles Sumner, and even Ulysses S. Grant; to events, like the Civil War and Reconstruction; to democracy itself, were determined by how these men, events, and that form of government affected the political fortunes of those whom he held most dear. Although Adams through this period had strong interests in history, literature, and art, politics permeated his existence.

In his earliest surviving letter, he repeated to his brother Charles Francis a conversation he had had with Richard Henry Dana—maritime lawyer, antislavery colleague of Adams's father, and author of *Two Years Before the Mast.* Before leaving Boston at twenty to study abroad, Adams told Dana he hoped to study law when he returned and to "emigrate and practice at Saint Louis." Dana responded contemptuously that Adams "was looking towards politics" as a career. Later Adams conceded that perhaps Dana "was right. There are two things," he told Charles, "that seem to be at the bottom of our constitutions; one is a continual tendency towards politics; the other is family pride; and it is strange how these two feelings run through all of us." Adams, however, insisted that he had not planned on politics, that he had "seen altogether too much harm done in this way, to allow myself to quit law for politics without irresistible reasons."[1]

"Irresistible reasons" quickly appeared. Believing in an "irrepressible conflict," Adams hoped that William Henry Seward would be "quietly elected President" in 1860 and consequently "comparatively conservative men" would be conducting and

---

[1] Adams (HA) to Charles Francis Adams, Jr. (CFA2), 3 Nov. 1858, J.C. Levenson, Ernest Samuels, et al., eds., *The Letters of Henry Adams, 1858–1892,* 3 vols. (Cambridge, Mass., 1982), 1: 4–5. Since all letters hereafter cited in this essay are in this collection it will be referred to simply by volume number and page.

controlling the antislavery movement. And if his father, a Massachusetts congressman, could weather the inevitable crisis, Adams predicted that Charles Francis Adams, Sr., "has a good chance of living in the White House some day. All depends on the ability he shows as a leader now. . . . If all goes right, the house of Adams may get it's lease of life renewed—if, as I've various times remarked, it has the requisite ability still."[2]

While Adams remained abroad until the fall of 1860, his attraction to politics grew stronger, particularly since his father was a leader in Congress and close to Seward. "Keep him allied with papa," Henry urged his mother, "the nearer the better. If he comes in as President in that case, we shall see fun." When he received word that his father was named chair of the Committee on Manufactures, a pleased Adams wrote home, "I had expected something of the sort, and yet was much gratified at this first national recognition of him as a power. It's pleasant to feel that we're going up the ladder still, and that nearly a hundred years hasn't exhausted the family yet." The Seward connection, however, was crucial, and Adams worried that he might not be nominated. "But damn the thing without Seward," he exclaimed. "I shall reserve all my penny-whistle for him." As the election approached and Republican optimism grew, Adams hoped that his brother Charles would "make quite a thing" of writing campaign "letters to some paper. . . . The truth is, we can't help it. It must out. This taste for politics is a perfect mania in us."[3]

In the fall of 1860 Henry Adams returned to Boston, began to study law, voted for Abraham Lincoln, and soon dropped law to accompany his family to Washington. There, during the great secession winter, he was secretary to his congressman father, tutored his sister Mary and brother Brooks, and represented his family at social functions. "It's a great life"; Adams wrote his brother Charles, "just what I wanted; and as I always feel that I am of real use here and can take an active part in it all, it never tires. Politically there is a terrible panic. . . . Seward is great; a perfect giant in all this howling. Our father is firmer that Mt Ararat." Adams feared that if the South were willing to compromise and use secession as a bargaining chip, it could gain concessions from "weak brethren" and completely disorganize the Republican party. "Our only hope," he believed, was that the South would probably "kick us out and refuse everything."[4]

[2]HA to CFA2, 23 Nov. 1859, 1: 67.
[3]HA to Abigail Brooks Adams, 13 Feb., 4 Mar., 7 Sept. 1860, 1: 92, 96–97, 201; HA to CFA2, 19 May 1860, 1: 149.
[4]HA to CFA2, 9, 13 Dec. 1860, 1: 204–207.

The South was intransigent, and though the union was disrupted the Republican party was preserved. The South refused to accept the firm but moderate policy of Seward and Charles Francis Adams, which would both contain and guarantee slaveholding where it existed. In that winter of uncertainties—union or disunion, war or peace, slavery extended or contained—Henry Adams, like his father, tried to keep cool. "I feel in a continual intoxication in this life," he exulted. "It is magnificent to feel strong and quiet in all this row, and see one's own path clear through all the chaos." With speculation rampant, Adams, despite his alleged coolness, repeated things that were wild and things that were prophetic. Convinced that the South was beyond conciliation, he expected that "a new Northern Union" with "a new Capital on the Mississippi" would be established, and he felt certain that if Virginia seceded war would follow.[5]

The "temporizing policy" of his elders was "hard work" and Adams was "sick of it," but moderation had achieved some success. Although Charles Sumner and other abolitionist-minded Republicans were unhappy, the party remained united and secession was limited to the cotton states of the Deep South. "The ancient Seward," Adams reported, "is in high spirits and chuckles himself hoarse with his stories. He says it's all right. We shall keep the border states and in three months or thereabouts, if we hold off, the Unionists and Disunionists will have their hands on each others throats in the cotton states. The storm is weathered."[6]

Seward was wrong; the storm had just begun. After South Carolina fired on Fort Sumter, unionist sentiment was almost nonexistent in the cotton South, powerless in most of the upper South, and even with federal support barely held its own in the border states. A formidable southern confederacy fought for the liberty to enslave millions.

Lincoln did not include Charles Francis Adams in his cabinet, but named him minister to Great Britain. Tagging along as his father's private secretary, Henry Adams stayed abroad for seven years. During this period, he remained intensely interested in both American and British politics. While the Civil War raged, his main concern was international politics, centering on his father's efforts to keep the British from mediating between the Union and the Confederacy and to prevent the sailing of British-built vessels designed either to destroy American commerce or to lift the Union blockade.   *14 8,326*

---

[5]HA to CFA2, 8, 11 Jan., 5 Feb. 1861, 1: 219–221, 228.
[6]HA to CFA2, 8 Feb. 1861, 1: 230.

To keep England neutral, Adams recognized the importance of federal military victories and the necessity of converting a nationalistic war of unification into a humanitarian crusade against slavery. In January 1862 he told Seward's son, who was his father's assistant secretary of state: "If some real emancipation step could be taken, it would be the next best thing to taking Richmond for us here." Adams also was an early advocate of recruiting black soldiers. "I assure you," he told his brother Charles, "that the strongest means of holding Europe back is the sight of an effective black army."[7]

Adams had no charity for the foe and advocated a harsh reconstruction policy. Arguing "there can be no peace on our continent so long as the southern people exist," Adams insisted, "We must exterminate them in the end, be it long or be it short, for it is a battle between us and slavery." Although Adams thought emancipation had to be gradual, he anticipated a long-term military occupation and colonization of the South by northern whites in alliance with southern blacks. This occupation would sap the strength of the slaveholders, expiate "the old crime," and reconstruct the "whole social system" by fostering "new industry and free institutions."[8]

The British aristocracy's sympathy for the Confederacy irked Adams, despite his close friendships with some aristocrats. He gloried that American democracy was the model of the future, believed "that our system and the English system are mortal enemies," and rejoiced with Lincoln's reelection in 1864. Not only would the Union be preserved, but the democratic process had triumphed. So confident in American democracy was Adams that he believed "a new era of the movement of the world will date from that [election] day."[9]

With the end of the war, Adams focused more on American politics and how he could influence it. Keenly aware of the importance of public opinion, he had dreamed during the war of shaping the postwar world. "But what we want, my dear boy," he outlined to Charles, "is a *school*. We want a national set of young men like ourselves . . . to start new influences not only in politics, but in literature, in law, in society, and throughout the whole social organism of the country."[10]

---

[7]HA to Frederick William Seward, 30 Jan. 1862, 1: 275; HA to CFA2, 19 July 1862, 1: 308.

[8]HA to CFA2, 16 May, 5 Sept. 1862, 1: 299, 309–310.

[9]HA to CFA2, 1 May 1863, 10 June, 25 Nov. 1864, 1: 350, 436, 458.

[10]HA to John Gorham Palfrey, 27 Mar. 1863, 1: 340; HA to CFA2, 21 Nov. 1862, 1: 315.

Though he wanted to come back to America, Henry Adams remained abroad during much of the troubled Andrew Johnson administration. Rather than shape events, he was left to grumble
at their rapid march, which left his family almost powerless.
Among those in high places, Adams complained, "We have not
one friend" except Seward. In eclipse, conservative Republicans,
whom Charles Francis Adams had led before the war, were
forced to support either Johnson or the dominant Radical wing
of the Republican party. With his family's political fortunes tied
to conservatives, Henry Adams forgot his radical wish to exterminate the slaveholding South and construct a new social system. In July 1865 he thought most Republicans at home were
"in an amusing provincial hurry to get into opposition" against
Johnson, who would allow the former slaveholders to rule the
South and maintain the supremacy of the white race. "Why so
fast? We have done with slavery. Free opinion, education and law
have now entrance into the south. . . . Let us give time; it doesn't
matter much how long. I doubt about black states. I fancy white
is better breeding stock."[11]

Adams hoped that a combination of conservative Republicans
and Democrats could defeat Radical Republicans. Aware in August 1866 that his "father is again in a miserable minority in Massachusetts, without a friend to work with," Adams found the
Radical Republican majority in Congress "violating the rights of
minorities [southern whites] more persistently than the worst
pro-slavery Congress ever could do" and violating the Constitution as well. A Radical setback at the polls in 1866 would restore
the Adams clan to power in the Republican party. These hopes of
Henry Adams were dashed by Johnson's intemperate stump
speeches against the Radicals and by an overwhelming Radical
triumph. "We are all back again as Republicans, our conspiracy
having failed. Let us now wait and see the new issue."[12]

Adams conceded that Johnson "may be an object of supreme
contempt," but he continued to fume against Radical Reconstruction. In this way he steered a course between his oldest brother
John Quincy Adams II, who supported Johnson and joined the
Democrats, and his older brother Charles Francis, who reluc-
tantly went along with the Radicals. Henry Adams declared: "I
reserve to myself as my most valued right, the privilege of attack-
ing all parties and following none." Nevertheless he was pleased

---

[11]HA to CFA2, 10 May, 14 July 1865, 1: 496, 498.
[12]HA to John Gorham Palfrey, 23 Aug. 1866, 1: 509; HA to CFA2, 10 Nov. 1866, 1: 512.

by the stands taken by John and Charles and admitted, like a pragmatic politician, that "from a narrower and perhaps from a lower point, I think it advisable to entertain relations with each side, and do not want to see the whole family on either."[13]

In the summer of 1868 Adams returned to the United States, after an absence of seven years, and in October moved to Washington, D.C. Having embarked on an "experiment," he was in an optimistic frame of mind. He set up shop as an independent political critic—an investigative journalist—tied to neither party, with close friends in both the outgoing Johnson and the incoming Grant administrations. Employed by no paper, he contributed primarily to the weekly *Nation* and the quarterly *North American Review*. With his friends in high places providing access to data, his capacity for work, and his slashing style, Adams through his articles became a leader among the reformers favoring a return to the gold standard, free trade, and civil service reform. From the moment he arrived in Washington, Adams hobnobbed with men like Attorney General William M. Evarts, Commissioner of the Revenue David A. Wells, his deputy Francis A. Walker, and Congressman James A. Garfield. Adams hoped these friends would also play a major role in the Grant administration.[14]

Contemplating recent developments while waiting for the advent of Ulysses S. Grant impressed Adams with the enormous job he had undertaken. He concluded that "our people may be properly divided into two classes, one which steals, the other which is stolen from"; that the "whole root of the evil is in *political* corruption"; and that "our coming struggle is going to be harder than the anti-slavery fight, and though we may carry free-trade, I fear we shall be beaten on the wider field."[15]

The corrosive effect of corruption—or of his family's lack of power—ate away at Adams's faith in democracy, a faith he had emphatically expressed in 1864. It also undermined his hopes for Grant. Adams failed to see how a "mere change" of administration would counteract corruption. This change, he thought,

will only improve our affairs so far as to make the system endurable, and so blind our people to the necessity of true reform. The idea that democracy in itself, by the mere fact of giving power to the masses, will elevate and purify human nature, seems to me to have now turned out

---

[13]HA to CFA2, 1 Mar., 3 Apr., 8 May 1867, 21 Apr. 1868, 1: 524, 528, 533, 570; HA to John Quincy Adams II, 2 Mar. 1867, 1: 525.
[14]HA to CFA2, 18 Jan. 1869, 2: 11–12.
[15]HA to Edward Atkinson, 1 Feb. 1869, 2: 15.

one of those flattering fictions which have in all ages deluded philan-
thropists. The great problem of every system of Government has been to
place administration and legislation in the hands of the best men. We
have tried our formula and find that it has failed in consequence of its
clashing with our other fundamental principle that one man is as good
as another.

Still unaware, like everyone else, of who would be in Grant's cabinet, Adams told Charles, "We here look for a reign of western
mediocrity, but perhaps one appreciates least the success of the
steamer, when one lives in the engine-room."[16]
    Having lowered his expectations, Adams was not as disillu-
sioned by Grant's cabinet as he claimed in the *Education*. The
"home appointments"—particularly George S. Boutwell, who
was "not a Wells man," to the Treasury Department—were not
satisfactory. "I am afraid," he told Charles, "there is more favor-
itism than public good in them. It's the old game with fresh
cards. But we are in the boat and have got to stay there." After
two weeks, Adams was "even more puzzled than astonished" by
Grant's behavior. He still predicted success in the long run if
Grant was intelligent, but Adams was beginning to doubt the capacity of Grant's mind.[17]
    After a month and a half of Grant, Adams declared that
everything (apart from his liver ailment, which extensive walks
had cured)

has gone wrong. My hopes of the new Administration have all been disappointed; it is far inferior to the last. My friends have almost all lost
ground instead of gaining it as I had hoped. My family is buried politically beyond recovery for years. I am becoming more and more isolated
so far as allies go. I even doubt whether I can find an independent organ
to publish my articles, so strong is the current against us.

A few days later, he told Charles, "I can't get you an office. The
only members of this Government that I have met are mere acquaintances, not friends, and I fancy no request of mine would be
likely to call out a gush of sympathy."[18]
    Nevertheless Adams relished his situation. He was obligated to
no one, and could "express pretty energetic opinions all round."

---

[16]HA to John Gorham Palfrey, 19 Feb. 1869, 2: 18–19; HA to CFA2, 23 Feb. 1869, 2: 20.
[17]HA to CFA2, 11, 29 Mar. 1869, 2: 21–22.
[18]HA to Charles Milnes Gaskell (CMG), 19 Apr. 1869, 2: 25; HA to CFA2, 29 Apr. 1869,
2: 26.

He felt even better when his *North American Review* article on the recent session of Congress was enthusiastically received, and vowed to "make my annual 'Session' an institution and a power in the land." In the article Adams insisted that "a decent self-respect should oblige Congress to show or feign some disposition to purge the civil service from the taint of political corruption." To his aristocratic English friend Charles Milnes Gaskell he boasted, "For once I have smashed things generally and really exercised a distinct influence on public opinion by acting on the limited number of cultivated minds."[19]

Despite his lamentations, Adams still had friends in the administration and in Congress, and he continued to publish articles in the *New York Evening Post* and the *Nation*. He met with Wells and Garfield in the summer of 1869 to plan their strategy and published an article in the October 1869 *North American Review* on civil service reform. Adams proudly described this article as "very bitter and abusive of the Administration. I expect," he continued, "to get into hot water, but have nothing to lose."[20]

Although the article charged that Grant carried the rotation of government employees in and out of office to a new extreme, it did not get Adams into trouble, perhaps because it took a different tack from that taken by most civil service reformers. Reform to Adams meant wresting back the executive's appointing power, which Congress had usurped. Adams suggested that the president lead the reform effort by issuing executive orders that would promote permanent tenure for officers, rather than have Congress, as most reformers demanded, create an independent commission to administer competitive examinations to applicants for office.

Adams's article not only outlined a method of civil service reform, but also revealed why he and his friends had become civil service reformers. Although they wanted good government, their concern for reform, Adams showed, had resulted primarily from loss of political power. He illustrated this underlying cause for reform by contrasting Attorney General Ebenezer Rockwood Hoar with Secretary of the Treasury George S. Boutwell—a contrast that the *Nation* applauded. Boutwell, Adams stated, was "the product of caucuses and party promotion." but Hoar was

---

[19]HA to CMG, 19 Apr., 17 May 1869, 2: 25, 31–32; HA to CFA2, 17 May 1869, 2: 30; HA, "The Session," *North American Review*, 108: 618.

[20]HA to CMG, 27 Aug. 1869, 2: 43.

by birth and by training a representative of the best New England school, holding his moral rules on the sole authority of his own conscience, indifferent to opposition whether in or out of his party, obstinate to excess, and keenly alive to the weaknesses in which he did not share. Judge Hoar belonged in fact to a class of men who had been gradually driven from politics, but whom it is the hope of reformers to restore. Mr. Boutwell belonged to the class which has excluded its rival, but which has failed to fill with equal dignity the place it has usurped.[21]

Adams hoped that Secretary of the Interior Jacob Dolson Cox would convince the cabinet and Grant to achieve permanent tenure by making no removals without cause. Adams urged Cox to "give the country a lead! We are wallowing in the mire for want of a leader. If the Administration will only frame a sound policy of reform, we shall all gravitate towards it like iron-filings to a magnet."[22]

By December 1869 Adams was pleased to report:

I am actually winding myself up in a coil of political intrigue and getting the reputation of a regular conspirator. My progess in a year has alarmed me, for it is too rapid to be sound. I am already deeper in the confidence of the present Government than I was with the last, although that was friendly and this a little hostile. It seems a little strange that after the violent attack I made on it . . . there should be no soreness, but the fact is, nearly every member of the Cabinet is in perfect sympathy with me in abusing themselves. You see there is a clear line of division in the Cabinet, and I am on the side which has the strongest men, and Reform is always a sure card.[23]

Adams was both right and wrong. He was right about his progress being too rapid to be sound and wrong about the rest. By February 1870 he recognized that in the struggle between reform and spoils politicians his side was "undermost," and by spring he knew that his friends in the cabinet were losing ground. Adams then gave up on the Grant administration and began working "with another set of men, strong in the press, but weak in power. We despise all the people in control, and all we can do is only to make a little more noise. So we are going into the elections next November. . . ." Adams aimed at "the splitting

---

[21]HA, "Civil-Service Reform," *North American Review*, 109: 443–475; "The North American Review for October," *Nation*, 9: 415.

[22]HA to Jacob Dolson Cox (JDC), 8 Nov. 1869, 2: 50–51.

[23]HA to CMG, 7 Dec. 1869, 2: 54.

of the majority and the practical formation of a new party on the issue" of "revenue reform, free trade and what not" and he smelled success when a dozen "leaders" met in his rooms and "effected a close alliance." He followed up that meeting by playing host on 18 April to a "political convention of half the greatest newspaper editors in the country."[24]

The exodus of reformers from Washington influenced Adams to become an assistant history professor at Harvard in the fall of 1870, although he hated Boston and loved Washington. "All my friends," Adams wrote, "have been or are on the point of being driven out of the government and I should have been left without any allies or sources of information. As it is, I only retire with the rest and leave our opponents to upset themselves, which they will do in time, I think, and when I go back there, it will be to study a new situation."[25]

Henry Adams had also taken on the *North American Review,* which, he told David A. Wells, he proposed to make "a regular organ of our opinions." Adams soon boasted: "The retirement from Washington has by no means thrown me out of politics. On the contrary, as editor I am deeper in them than ever, and my party is growing so rapidly that I look forward to the day when we shall be in power again as not far distant." Since the administration had suffered a setback in the fall 1870 elections (particularly with the success of Liberal Republicans in Missouri), Adams's prediction was not based entirely on fancy.[26]

Although composed of reform elements disappointed by the Grant administration, Adams's group continued to work within the Republican party for free trade and civil service reform. In late November Adams and about twenty other editors and reformers met to lay "vast and ambitious projects for the future." Since James G. Blaine, Speaker of the House, had "pledged himself to give us the Committee of Ways and Means, and any other positions that might be required of him," the group "determined to support Blaine on the avowed ground that he had become one of us" and not "to use the 'new party' except as a threat, for the present." If Blaine and Congress did not embrace reform, the new party would issue a call for a convention in the spring. The reform group considered the Grant administration "broken down—and our only doubt," Adams insisted, "was whether it was best to break the party down too, or to put it on its good behavior. As for

---

[24]HA to CMG, 20 Feb., 28 Mar., 3, 29 Apr. 1870, 2: 64, 67–69.
[25]HA to CMG, 25 Oct. 1870, 2: 84.
[26]HA to David A. Wells (DAW), 25 Oct. 1870, 2: 85; HA to CMG, 19 Nov. 1870, 2: 89.

doubt of our own power, I was amused to see how little there was of it."[27]

Despite the arrogance of the reformers, the Grant administration was far from broken down. Although Adams claimed that anarchy ruled the nation, the administration moved to undermine the reformers. In his December 1870 annual message, Grant embraced civil service reform, and in March 1871 Congress empowered him to appoint a commission to prescribe rules for examining applicants. By June Grant named a commission with George William Curtis at its head, and on 1 January 1872 its rules, promulgated by Grant, went into effect.[28]

These moves divided reformers. Moderate ones, like Curtis, continued to support Grant and his party, while intense reformers, like Adams, opposed the administration. "We are," he complained in September 1871, "rapidly subsiding into political indifferentism if we are not already there. Our reforms are not advancing, so far as I can see."[29]

Even Adams was neglecting politics in late 1871 and early 1872. He had become engaged to Marian Hooper, whom friends and family called "Clover." But 1872 was a presidential election year and beginning in January the stop-Grant, Liberal Republican movement gathered momentum, and Charles Francis Adams was the odds-on favorite to receive its nomination. Henry Adams on 27 April 1872 confessed that:

Love . . . though an amusing pastime, . . . is by no means the only matter of concern to me . . . for a new presidential canvass is beginning and all the elements of discontent with the present administration have agreed to meet at Cincinnati next week and strike hands. The gathering will be tremendous and my old political friends are deep in it. We do not know what will be done there, but as yet my father commands much the most powerful support for the nomination, and it is not improbable that all parties may combine on him. If so, there will be the most exasperating election that has taken place for years, and one of which it is impossible to guess the result. Of course I keep out of it with great care, and am glad to be off to Europe,

where Adams and Clover planned to go on their honeymoon. Although he thought it "well enough" for his father to be president, he professed to look "with great equanimity" on the possibility of

[27]HA to JDC, 28 Nov. 1870, 2: 91–92; HA to CMG, 19 Dec. 1870, 2: 95.
[28]HA to Charles Eliot Norton, 13 Jan. 1871, 2: 97; Ari Hoogenboom, *Outlawing the Spoils: A History of the Civil Service Reform Movement, 1865–1883* (Urbana, 1961), 85–96.
[29]HA to JDC, 30 Sept. 1871, 2: 116.

the choice falling upon another. Clover, however, wanted to be the daughter-in-law of the president.[30]

To the chagrin of the reformers, and particularly of the Adams clan, the convention nominated the editor of the *New York Tribune*, Horace Greeley. He was the foremost advocate of a protective tariff, a friend of the spoils system, and widely regarded as a crackpot intrinsically unfit for the presidency. Adams exclaimed, "If the Gods insist on making Mr. Greeley our President, I give it up. Otherwise all is dark as Erebus." When he was asked to write for Greeley's paper a series of articles on the objections of Liberal Republicans to Grant's renomination, Adams declined with the excuse that he was going abroad.[31]

Grant was renominated and overwhelmingly defeated Greeley, whom the Democrats also supported. The campaign was disastrous for reformers, who split three ways. Moderates consistently supported Grant, some Liberal Republicans swallowed Greeley's nomination without regurgitating, and other Liberal Republicans, who detested Grant and despised Greeley, either voted for Grant or did not vote. Over the next three years, reformers, whom Adams considered to be "in a very bad way," failed to work together.[32]

During Grant's second term, Adams viewed politics as "contemptible to the last degree." But the more politics went "to the dogs," the more people were aroused, and as the prospects for the reformers improved in early 1875 Adams's spirit soared. He reported to his English friend Gaskell that he was "carrying on no end of political intrigues," leading mankind by the nose, and losing his

self-respect in this underhand work of pulling wires. . . . Just now I am engaged single-handed in the slight task of organising a new party to contest the next Presidential election in '76. As yet I have only three allies; a broken down German politician [Carl Schurz]; a newspaper correspondent [Horace White], and a youth of twenty [Henry Cabot Lodge] who is to do all the work. With these instruments I propose to do no less than decide the election of 1876. You will see.[33]

Adams managed to reunite bickering reformers. A dinner honoring Schurz on his retirement from the Senate provided the oc-

[30]HA to CMG, 14, 21 Dec. 1871, 27 Apr. 1872, 2: 123, 135.
[31]HA to CMG, 30 May 1872, 2: 137; HA to Whitelaw Reid, 15 May 1872, 2: 136.
[32]HA to CMG, 13 Feb. 1874, 2: 188.
[33]HA to CMG, 22 June 1874, 15 Feb. 1875, 2: 193–194, 217.

casion for a "*demonstration*," which Adams justifiably boasted "was originated, hatched and generally brought into life by me as a result of six months incubation." The newspapers assumed correctly that the object of the "new party" was to make Charles Francis Adams president. Henry Adams pretended to oppose the idea, lest "we shall all shipwreck on that rock. Nevertheless," he told Gaskell,

we shall go ahead and you need not be surprised to hear that we have covered ourselves with eternal ridicule by some new absurd failure, or have subsided into nothing for sheer feebleness, or have actually effected a brilliant *coup*, brought our man in as President, and are the rulers of forty million people. Such is the chaotic condition of our politics that any of these results is possible. Of course it indicates that our whole political fabric is out of joint and running wild, but so it is. My scheme is to organise a party of the centre and to support the party which accepts our influence most completely. But I doubt whether we can absolutely overthrow both parties as many of our ardent friends seem almost inclined to try doing.[34]

In the fall of 1875 the outcome of the Ohio gubernatorial election confirmed Adams's hope that his movement held the balance of power. Rutherford B. Hayes, a sound-money, respectable Republican, aided by the campaigning of Schurz, defeated the inflationist Democratic incumbent by five thousand votes. "Narrow enough," said Adams, "but every man in that five thousand is one of us. You will hear more of us next year. We will play for high stakes and have nothing to lose."[35]

By February 1876 Adams was less optimistic.

Our organisation has been secretly effected and is ready to act, but is in doubt what it ought to do and although we have unquestionably the power to say that any given man shall not be President, we are not able to say that any given man shall be President. Our first scheme was to force my father on the parties. This is now abandoned, and . . . we mean to support the present Secretary of the Treasury, [Benjamin H.] Bristow, for the Presidency.

Adams was uneasy. "I am no longer confident of doing good and am looking with anxiety to the future." He admitted that

---

[34]HA to CMG, 24 May 1875, 2: 225–226.
[35]HA to CMG, 4, 15 Oct. 1875, 2: 239–240.

"things are getting beyond my capacity to influence or even to measure."[36]

Adams's main concern was to hold the Independents together. "Whatever support is given to Mr. Bristow or to anyone else, it is all important that we should act ultimately as a unit, and that the certainty of this ultimate action should be the cardinal point of our tactics." A loyal Republican, Bristow refused to run as an Independent, and Schurz rejected Adams's idea for a meeting of Independents after, rather than before, the major party conventions. Complaining that "Bristow's friends are cutting his and our throats," and that the Independents "have no leader nor organisation," Adams vowed to give up trying to better the times.[37]

Although discouraged, Adams refused to give up completely. Just before the Republican convention, he had "*no* real hope" that Bristow would be nominated, but he thought "the democrats might yet help us through" in their convention. Rather than Bristow, Rutherford B. Hayes, whom Adams had championed for governor of Ohio, got the nomination, and Adams was disappointed. "We organised our party," he wrote, "and as usual have been beaten. After our utmost efforts we have only succeeded in barring the road to our opponents and forcing them to nominate as candidate for the Presidency one Hayes of Ohio, a third-rate nonentity whose only recommendation is that he is obnoxious to no one. I hope to enjoy the satisfaction of voting against him." Even though Adams soon realized that Hayes had reform sympathies and deserved support if elected, Adams backed the Democratic nominee, Samuel Jones Tilden.[38]

Adams's "real object" was not to elect Tilden or Hayes but "to increase the independent power." Adams was particularly annoyed with Schurz for not helping him gain this objective. "Console yourself about politics," he wrote Henry Cabot Lodge.

You are indeed the one who has the best right to complain, for you had the most trouble in forming that rope of sand, the independent party. I cannot help laughing to think how, after all our labor and after we had by main force created a party for Schurz to lead, he himself, without a word or a single effort to keep his party together, kicked us over in his haste to jump back to the Republicans.

---

[36]HA to CMG, 9 Feb. 1876, 2: 247.
[37]HA to Carl Schurz, 14 Feb. 1876, 2: 250; HA to DAW, 20 Mar. 1876, 2: 262.
[38]HA to Henry Cabot Lodge (HCL), 27 May 1876, 2: 269; HA to CMG, 14 June 1876, 2: 276; HA to DAW, 15 July 1876, 2: 282.

If Blaine had been nominated, Adams believed, the Independents would have held together, but given the choice of Hayes or Tilden they "dissolved like a summer cloud." Adams was discouraged with his Independent party and tired of teaching and editing. "Satisfied that literature offers higher prizes than politics," he buried himself in the study of America's, and to a large degree his family's, past.[39]

Despite his comment in 1878 that "Even politics no longer interest us," Adams continued to comment on politics and to hob-nob with politicians. In 1881 Adams invested in the New York *Evening Post* not to make money, but to provide a forum for reform and as a way "of keeping in with my crowd." Asking merely that the *Post* be kept "steady," he neither wrote articles to shape public opinion nor attempted with his old vigor to organize the reform element.[40]

Although Adams was disappointed with the results of the Independent movement and derisively spoke of himself as "smiling at the ruins," his attempts to organize reformers were more effective than he admitted. In 1876 his movement forced the Republican party to nominate, not a spoilsman, but a reform-minded candidate and Adams himself called the Hayes administration "most successful." Adams also helped both to originate and to sustain the civil service reform movement. When in January 1883 Congressman John A. Kasson snarled at Adams, "Well, the House has passed your *Boston* bill," Kasson recognized the enormous contribution Henry Adams had made to the Pendleton Civil Service Reform Act. In politics, as in other areas, Adams's self-deprecating claims of failure obscure his solid accomplishments.[41]

---

[39]HA to HCL, 5 Aug., 4 Sept. 1876, 2: 285, 291; HA to CMG, 8, 30 Sept. 1876, 14 Apr. 1877, 2: 292, 303.

[40]HA to CMG, 6 Oct. 1878, 2: 346; HA to E.L. Godkin, 19 Sept. 1881, 2: 434. In 1883 Adams said he would "gladly help to organise a free trade party," but apparently made no further move. HA to Carl Schurz, 20 May 1883, 2: 503.

[41]HA to CMG, 8, 30 Sept. 1876, 2: 292; HA to HCL, 13 May 1880, 2: 400; HA to John Hay, 7 Jan. 1883, 2: 487.

HENRY ADAMS AND THE AMERICAN CENTURY

DAVID R. CONTOSTA

Nearly fifty years before Henry Luce wrote his famous essay, "The American Century," for *Life Magazine*, Henry Adams knew that the United States could soon dominate world affairs.[1] He also believed that his country might confront a dangerous rival in a post-revolutionary Russian empire. Although Adams was proud of America's growing might, he found the prospect of world hegemony unnerving, lest his countrymen prove unfit for their new role. These and other speculations over shifting balances of power at the turn of the century have made Adams one of the most profound critics of modern America.

Both by birth and experience, Adams was well qualified for the role of critic. The descendant of presidents and diplomats, Henry became the heir apparent to his family's public fortunes when his father, Charles Francis Adams, took him to London as private secretary following the elder Adams's appointment as minister to Great Britain in 1861.[2] In fact, Henry became something of an unofficial assistant minister, who helped in numerous ways with sensitive negotiations during the American Civil War.

Returning home after the war, Henry lacked the political base to command a diplomatic post of his own. Yet his professional activities and important personal connections over the next half century would amplify his understanding of geopolitics and international relations. His nine-volume *History of the United States during the Administrations of Thomas Jefferson and James Madison*, for example, provided insights into international power politics on a gigantic scale.[3] He told of Napoleon's colossal defeat, of Great Britain's emergence as the world's premier power, and of his own

---

[1]Henry R. Luce, "The American Century," *Life* 17 February 1941, pp. 61–65.

[2]The best biography of Charles Francis Adams is Martin Duberman, *Charles Francis Adams* (Stanford, 1960).

[3]Henry Adams, *History of the United States During the Administrations of Thomas Jefferson and James Madison* (New York, 1889–1891), 9 vols. The most recent edition is a two-volume set published by the Library of America (New York, 1986).

country's second struggle for independence during the War of 1812. Equally important to his appreciation of world affairs was the salon that he and his wife Marian ("Clover") Adams held from the late 1870s in their house in Washington, D.C., across the street from the White House on Lafayette Square. From the first, invitations to the Adamses' late afternoon teas and intimate dinners were sought by statesmen and diplomats.[4]

The Adamses' closest friend in Washington during these years was John Hay, former assistant to President Lincoln, seasoned diplomat, man of letters, and later secretary of state under Presidents William McKinley and Theodore Roosevelt. As if to seal their friendship in mortar and stone, Adams and Hay commissioned adjoining houses on Lafayette Square in 1884, designed by Adams's architect friend, Henry Hobson Richardson. Whenever they were both in town, Adams and Hay took walks in the afternoon from four to five, returning together in time for tea. Even after Hay became secretary of state in 1898, their daily constitutionals continued, with Hay unburdening himself to Adams. Although Adams seldom hesitated to give advice, it remains unclear whether he had any direct influence on policy. Nevertheless, Adams often served as an unofficial "go-between," meeting with foreign envoys in his home and conveying their conversations to Hay. In this way, Adams maintained an insider's view of American foreign policy.[5]

Several events in the early 1890s drew Adams's attention more forcefully to the international scene than at any time since the Civil War. One was his round-the-world voyage with painter John La Farge in 1890–1892. Coming back to the West after more than a year in the South Pacific and Orient, he stopped in Paris for several months before continuing his journey home to Washington. His arrival in the French capital, after so long being out of touch with the West, jolted Adams's sensibilities and alerted him to important changes in French—and European life in general. It was also during this visit that he selected Paris as a window on the world. Until the outbreak of World War I in 1914 he made a regular habit of spending six to seven months of every year there.[6]

---

[4]On the Adams salon and their many friendships, see Patricia O'Toole, *The Five of Hearts: An Intimate Portrait of Henry Adams and His Friends, 1880–1918* (New York, 1990) and Ernest Scheyer, *The Circle of Henry Adams* (Detroit, 1970).

[5]An excellent biography of John Hay is Keaton J. Clymer's *John Hay* (Ann Arbor, Mich., 1975).

[6]For a consideration of Adams's debt to French life and culture see Max I. Baym, *The French Education of Henry Adams* (New York, 1951) and Robert Mane, *Henry Adams on the Road to Chartres* (Cambridge, Mass., 1971).

As he wrote in September 1895, "[Paris] is the only city in the world which understands the world and itself."[7]

It was the world-wide financial panic of the early 1890s, however, that riveted Adams's attention on international affairs and convinced him that economic realities were the driving force of all great-power rivalries. Commencing in Great Britain, the panic reached the United States in the summer of 1893 while Adams was in Switzerland with his close friends, U.S. Senator Donald Cameron and his beautiful wife, Elizabeth Sherman Cameron. An urgent telegram from his brothers sent Adams scurrying back across the Atlantic to the Adams homestead at Quincy, Massachusetts, where he helped to steady his brothers' nerves and salvage the family trust. Just as important were the lengthy discussions that summer and early autumn between Henry and his youngest brother Brooks. Brooks had already set down some forceful ideas about civilization, economic systems, and shifting balances of power in a long, unpublished essay. From this essay, and his protracted talks with Henry at Quincy, came Brooks's brilliant and controversial *Law of Civilization and Decay*, first published in 1895.[8]

Stripped of its refinements, Brooks's law held that the most important human motives were fear and greed. In the earliest stages of civilization, fear of the unknown and fear of injury from others, was the dominant human emotion. This fear found an outlet in religious belief and the martial spirit, both of which offered security against real or imagined enemies. During later stages of civilization fear gave way to material greed, a craving for superfluous wealth that also flowed from a desire to insulate oneself from real or fancied dangers. In this search for security, governments, religions, and financial organizations had tried to concentrate more and more power, over increasingly large areas of the globe. Such efforts had produced monotheistic religions, larger and more powerful governments, and, most recently, huge commercial and financial monopolies.

Henry did not accept every detail of Brooks's theory and in a letter to his brother, written in April 1898, he attempted to restate the law of civilization and decay in its simplest terms. According to Henry's version of the law,

All Civilization is Centralization.
All Centralization is Economy.

---

[7]Henry Adams to Elizabeth Cameron, 12 September 1895, in *Letters of Henry Adams*, edited by J. C. Levenson et al. (Cambridge, Mass., 1988), 4: 324.

[8]On Henry's brother Brooks, see Thornton Anderson, *Brooks Adams: Constructive Conservative* (Ithaca, N.Y., 1951) and Arthur F. Beringause, *Brooks Adams: A Biography* (New York, 1955). An examination of the intellectual relationship between the two brothers is Timothy Paul Donovan, *Henry Adams and Brooks Adams* (Norman, Okla., 1961).

Therefore all Civilization is the survival of the most economical (cheapest).[9]

Henry did not always use this formula to explain foreign relations in the late nineteenth and early twentieth centuries, but there were several elements of it that made sense to him in the contemporary world: The principal motives of the great powers, he believed, were fear and greed. The main impetus of international rivalries was therefore the struggle among governments to concentrate greater political and economic power than their competitors. Because certain natural and cultural advantages accrued to different countries at different stages in history, some states would rise while others declined, a process that produced international tensions and often war.[10]

As Adams viewed the international scene at the turn of the century, the United States was a rising power, while certain European countries, and especially Great Britain, were on the wane. A comparison of both human and natural resources, along with a series of international events between 1895 and 1918, convinced him of this trend.

The first of these happenings was the so-called Venezuelan crisis of 1895, during which the United States and Great Britain nearly went to war over the boundary between Venezuela and British Guiana. Despite his life-long Anglophobia, Adams did not believe that war with Great Britain was in American national interests. It was only a matter of time until British authority in the Western Hemisphere came to an end, and the United States asserted its influence throughout the New World. He was also convinced that this could occur both gradually and peacefully.[11]

The Cuban Revolution, which also broke out in 1895, was a different matter for Adams. Lying just ninety miles from the Florida coast, Cuba was of great strategic importance to the United States, a fact that had not been lost on Henry's grandfather, John Quincy Adams. In addition, Henry was very sympathetic toward the Cuban rebels and their struggle for independence against Spain.

Adams's personal connection with the Cuban rebels began during his first visit to Cuba in the winter of 1893, accompanied by his close friend Clarence King.[12] King, who was an accomplished

---

[9]Henry Adams to Brooks Adams, 2 April 1898, *Letters*, 4: 557.

[10]Adams's analysis of the rise and decline of world powers is amazingly similar to that put forth in the late 1980s by Paul Kennedy in his *Rise and Fall of the Great Powers* (New York, 1987), xv-xxv.

[11]For example, see Henry Adams to Brooks Adams, 5 June 1895, *Letters*, 4: 282–285.

[12]Adams to John Hay, 24 February 1893 and Adams to Elizabeth Cameron, 23 February and 28 February 1893, *Letters*, 4: 88–91.

geologist, writer, and hopeless romantic, had a knack for getting along with native peoples. Not long after their arrival in Cuba, King befriended a group of future rebel leaders and became, along with Adams, an outspoken convert to their cause. When the revolution broke out in 1895, Adams was one of the warmest American supporters of the rebel movement, even to the point of opening his house on Lafayette Square to the Cuban junta. As Adams's biographer Ernest Samuels put it, "Adams's house was now a hotbed of Cuban intrigue. He pulled every wire within reach trying to line up congressional support. . . ."[13]

Helpful in Adams's Cuban campaign was his friend Donald Cameron, a member of the Senate Foreign Relations Committee. Sympathetic, too, was Elizabeth Cameron's uncle, Senator John Sherman, who chaired the Foreign Relations Committee. Cameron invited Adams to write a committee report, submitted under the senator's name, which called for direct American intervention on behalf of the rebels. Although the committee unanimously approved the report, President Grover Cleveland opposed the resolution and the committee decided against bringing it before the full Senate for debate.[14]

Adams hoped for Cuban independence without war between the United States and Spain, but he supported the conflict once it came. Yet he was troubled by the American decision to annex the Philippine Islands. He used all the influence he could muster to convince Congress and the McKinley administration to grant the islands their independence, but to no avail.[15] When the Filipinos rebelled against American occupation forces, touching off a bloody three-year conflict, Adams was sickened. To Elizabeth Cameron he wrote in January 1899, "I turn green in bed at midnight if I think of the horror of a year's warfare in the Philippines. . . ."[16]

Forcing American rule upon the Filipinos was for Adams a flagrant violation of his country's own revolutionary heritage, "contrary to every profession or so-called principle of our lives and history."[17] More importantly, annexation of the Philippines was not in the national interest: the United States would have to govern a territory that was hard to defend and that could lead to friction and even war with another of the great powers. Equally

---

[13]Ernest Samuels, *Henry Adams: The Major Phase* (Cambridge, Mass., 1964), 163.
[14]Ibid., 173; Adams to Elizabeth Cameron, 29 November 1898, *Letters*, 4: 625–628.
[15]Adams to Elizabeth Cameron, 4 December 1898, *Letters*, 4: 629–631.
[16]Adams to Elizabeth Cameron, 22 January 1899, *Letters*, 4: 670.
[17]Ibid.

alarming, the United States faced the same difficulties as other imperial governments, with a sullen and resentful people to govern halfway around the globe.[18] The war with Japan between 1941 and 1945, the Japanese conquest of the Philippines, and the American reconquest of these islands later gave a terrible credibility to Adams's warnings.

Although unhappy about the Philippine annexation, Adams could see the Spanish-American War and its aftermath as proof that the balance of world power was undergoing a massive shift. His country's expulsion of Spain from the New World after four hundred years coincided with a return to prosperity in the United States and the beginning of a new century. Upon returning to Washington from Europe in January 1900, he wrote to his old English friend, Sir Robert Cunliffe, "I find America so cheerful, and so full of swagger and self-satisfaction, that I hardly know it."[19] A month later he wrote to his brother Brooks in the same vein: "From the moment of landing in New York, I was conscious of a change of scale. Our people seemed to swing at least twice the weight, twice as rapidly, and with only half the display of effort . . . ; the sense of energy is overpowering."[20]

The American century had begun just as the calendar was turning from the old century to the new, and even the frequently pessimistic Adams could not help but feel proud of his country's novel position in the world. At the same time he worried that this new power might lead to excesses by the United States. Caution should thus be the order of the day: "We are quietly cooling down about expansion," he observed to his young friend, Worthington Chauncey Ford, "and, if we react slowly and moderately, we shall come out somewhere on firm ground."[21] Meanwhile Adams believed that the United States must do everything in its power to keep the peace; for war was both profligate and unpredictable. As he insisted to Brooks, "War is always a blunder, necessarily stupid, and usually avoidable. Every ounce of energy put into it is three-fourths waste."[22]

Given his feelings about war, it is not surprising that Adams grew alarmed over increasing European tensions as the American century dawned. Everywhere the old ground seemed to rumble and shift, as some of the great powers slipped and others

---

[18]Adams to John Hay, 2 November 1901, *Letters*, 5: 302–304.
[19]Adams to Sir Robert Cunliffe, 25 January 1900, *Letters*, 5: 76.
[20]Adams to Brooks Adams, 7 February 1900, *Letters*, 5: 87.
[21]Adams to Worthington Chauncey Ford, 28 February 1899, *Letters*, 4: 697.
[22]Adams to Brooks Adams, 3 November 1901, *Letters*, 5: 305.

gained in strength. The major players in this dangerous game were Great Britain, Russia, Germany, and the United States.

The most alarming of these shifts was the decline of Great Britain. According to Adams the British Empire had become too large for the mother country to manage at a time when its economic position was being eroded by competition with the United States and Germany. Proof of this was found in Britain's trade figures, which Adams examined constantly, from information supplied to him by Worthington Chauncey Ford, former head of the Bureau of Statistics at the U.S. Treasury Department.

A more dramatic sign of Britain's declining fortunes was the Boer War of 1899–1902. At first Adams instinctively sided with the Boers, and in a long letter to John Hay he vented his fury against the British, who apparently had learned nothing from the American Revolution:

It is now two hundred years, or six generations, since these relations of mine undertook to teach the English how to manage a colony, and we thought we had succeeded at the cost of two wars, and two hundred years of preaching. We thought it was acknowledged that we were right, and that G[eorge] Washington was not a felon.[23]

Ever the realist, Adams put his prejudices aside when he concluded that a collapse of the British Empire would touch off a series of cataclysms. With only some exaggeration, he shared these thoughts on Britain's downfall with Hay:

To anyone who has all his life studied history, it is obvious that the fall of England would be paralleled by only two great convulsions in human record; the fall of the Roman Empire in the fourth century and the fall of the Roman Church in the sixteenth. Big as the catastrophe was when Spain went down, and France, neither was anything like England; they were small by comparison. Spain has taken at least two hundred years and a score of wars to founder completely. France has convulsed our century in doing so. For God's mercy, what will England do![24]

Adams well understood that one of the greatest threats to Britain during the early twentieth century was Germany. While often disgusted with Kaiser Wilhelm's bellicose posturings, he also knew that Germany's growing economic might would give it a greater role in world affairs, whether anyone liked it or not. Thus

---

[23]Adams to John Hay, 2 November 1901, *Letters*, 5: 302.
[24]Adams to John Hay, 4 December 1900, *Letters*, 5: 177.

when the first Moroccan crisis of 1905 threatened to touch off a general war, Adams could sympathize somewhat with the Germans and told Hay that the other powers should go out of their way to appease Germany in North Africa.[25] But he refused to exaggerate Germany's swagger, asserting that it was not large enough to take on the other powers by itself. Only some kind of political and economic consolidation (by force or otherwise) would allow Germany to dominate the European continent. The most likely candidate for absorption, Adams thought, was Russia, a supposition that was confirmed in both World War I and World War II, when Germany invaded its eastern neighbor.[26]

Dangerous though Germany appeared to be, Adams thought that Russia posed an even greater potential threat to international stability. He had long been a student of Alexis de Tocqueville's *Democracy in America*, and he must have known of Tocqueville's prediction that the United States and Russia would one day become contending superpowers. By the early twentieth century Adams could agree that his mentor was correct, given Russia's large population, vast territory, and abundant natural resources.

In order to investigate conditions first hand, Adams visited Russia with Henry Cabot Lodge and his wife Anna Cabot Mills Lodge in August 1901. Writing to Elizabeth Cameron, he exclaimed, "[Russia] dwarfs Europe instantly, by scale rather than mere size."[27] He realized that Russia was far behind in industry, estimating at one point that it was where the United States had been in 1870.[28] In order to realize its full potential as a nation, however, Russia would have to reform its entire political and economic system. In the process, Adams feared that Russia would pass through an upheaval as violent as the French Revolution more than a century before. "I am half crazy with fear," he confessed to Elizabeth Cameron, "that Russia is sailing straight into another French Revolution which may upset all Europe and us too."[29] For that reason, Adams was one of the few in Washington who favored Russia at the outset of the Russo-Japanese War of 1904–1905, supposing that a Russian defeat would throw the entire country and much of Europe into convulsions.

As with Great Britain, Adams believed that some sort of Russian disaster was in the offing and hoped that the crisis could be

[25]Adams to John Hay, 3 May 1905, *Letters*, 5: 650–651.
[26]Adams to John Hay, 7 November 1900, *Letters*, 5: 167–169.
[27]Adams to Elizabeth Cameron, 10 August 1901, *Letters*, 5: 276.
[28]Adams to Cecil Spring Rice, 31 May 1897, *Letters*, 4: 474–475; to John Hay, 11 January 1898, 6: 521–522; to Elizabeth Cameron, 1 September 1901, 5: 286–288.
[29]Adams to Elizabeth Cameron, 10 January 1904, *Letters*, 5: 539.

avoided for the sake of world peace. He found himself in the dilemma of wanting to maintain the status quo while realizing that certain changes might be constructive in the long run—as well as inevitable.[30] It was accordingly in his country's interest to have "a successful Russia, with a peaceful system," a wish that is as constructive to the United States in the late twentieth century as it was in 1905.[31]

Compared to Russia, China was not a great power by any measure. Yet Adams thought that the Chinese possessed great potential. At times he feared that the Russians might succeed in organizing and then dominating China, thereby achieving a higher level of concentration for both countries. If that happened—or if the Chinese themselves organized sufficiently—Adams believed that the United States would have a difficult time contending with them. "We never can compete with Asia," he wrote to Elizabeth Cameron in March 1903.[32] Given the recent rise of Japan, China, and Pacific rim, Adams's predictions are all the more intriguing.

Because of such potential shifts in the balance of power, Adams believed that war would be hard to avoid in the early twentieth century. In 1898 he had written, "A European war is mathematically certain."[33] Despite his pessimism, Adams would not give up on thinking about ways to achieve peace. One means, he thought, was a higher level of political and economic concentration in the West. What he had in mind was an "Atlantic Alliance."

The cornerstone of this alliance would be some sort of Anglo-American pact. Putting aside his hereditary animosity toward Britain, Adams applauded the Anglo-American rapprochement of the late nineteenth and early twentieth centuries, as represented by the Hay-Pauncefote treaties and the settlement of various boundary disputes.[34] Adams also wanted to detach France from an alliance with Russia that he took to be anti-British, although it became part of the Triple Entente. If possible, he would bring Germany into the Atlantic alliance. As he described his vision to Hay in May 1905,

We want our Atlantic system,—which extends from the Rocky Mountains, on the west, to the Elbe on the east, and develops nine tenths of

---

[30]Henry Adams, *The Education of Henry Adams* (Boston, 1918), 438–441.
[31]Adams to Charles Milnes Gaskell, 27 August 1904, *Letters*, 5: 606.
[32]Adams to Elizabeth Cameron, 22 March 1903, *Letters*, 5: 475.
[33]Adams to William W. Rockhill, 12 June 1898, *Letters*, 4: 601.
[34]Adams to Elizabeth Cameron, 12 February 1900 and 26 February 1900, *Letters*, 5: 90–93, 97–99.

the energy of the world. . . . . All western Germany is American, Atlantic and anti-military. We only need to work with it, and help it to what it thinks it wants; and above all, to remove, as far as we can, the inevitable friction with France and England.[35]

Tragically, the guns of August 1914 unleashed what Adams most dreaded—a European conflagration of unparalleled death and destruction. By then he had suffered his first serious stroke; a second massive stroke would kill him in March 1918. Yet he had lived long enough to see the American entry into World War I and had taken consolation in the close cooperation among Great Britain, France, and the United States. It took another World War to bring Germany into the Atlantic alliance, but Adams surely would have been pleased by the creation of NATO in 1949. The subsequent Cold War between NATO and the Soviet bloc would have disturbed him greatly, but the end of the Cold War and genuine international cooperation between the United States and the Soviet Union in the late 1980s would have brought a smile to his face.

Despite exaggerations and downright mistakes in judgment, Adams anticipated nearly every major shift in the international balance of power during the twentieth century, including those that transpired long after his death. That it turned out to be an American century would not have surprised him at all. As a man of peace, he would only hope that the newest constellations of power might make the last decade of the twentieth century a time of widespread harmony, prosperity, and peace.

---

[35]Adams to John Hay, 3 May 1905, *Letters*, 5: 651.

RELIGION AS CULTURE: HENRY ADAMS'S
MONT-SAINT-MICHEL AND CHARTRES

Alfred Kazin

The historian was thus reduced to his last resources. Clearly if he was bound to reduce all these forces to a common value, this common value could have no measure but that of their attraction on his own mind. He must treat them as they had been felt; as convertible, reversible, interchangeable attractions on thought.

> "The Dynamo and the Virgin"
> *The Education of Henry Adams*[1]

The largest memorial to Henry Adams is located, of all places, on the Upper West Side of New York, Amsterdam Avenue and 100th Street, just before the Hispanic *barrio* is replaced by Columbia University. The Cathedral of Saint John the Divine, really two churches in one and eclipsed in size only by St. Peter's in Rome, was on its present lines designed by Ralph Adams Cram, a fervent admirer of Adams's *Mont-Saint-Michel and Chartres*. The ideal of an American Episcopal cathedral had been suggested as early as 1828; the original design, Romanesque-Byzantine, went into the apse, choir, and crossing. Construction was remarkably slow, and in 1911, when the officiating bishop and the architects were dead, Cram, of the firm of Cram and Ferguson in Boston, was allowed to complete the church on Gothic principles.

Cram was passionate about Gothic, long convinced that Gothic had been the perfect expression of Western Christendom for five centuries and that Gothic had not died a natural death but had been cut off by the classicism of the Renaissance and the Protestant Revolution. The famous church-building firm of Cram and Goodhue was inspired by a compound of Pre-Raphaelitism and William Morris socialism, which foreshadowed the sentimental medievalism of G.K. Chesterton and Eric Gill, Wagner's *Parsifal*, and the arts and crafts movement opposing soulless technology. Cram himself was such a loving medievalist in the *Idylls of the*

---

[1]Henry Adams, *The Education of Henry Adams* (Boston, 1974), 383.

48

King style of the Victorian age that he collaborated in a magazine called *The Knight Errant*, composed *Excalibur: An Arthurian Drama*, and kept an ideal vision of the Middle Ages that is reflected in *The Gothic Quest* (1907), where he asked whether America wanted churches or meeting-houses. His firm designed the Gothic buildings at West Point (1903), which gave impetus to the spread of collegiate Gothic in the United States. It was said of Cram after he was baptized and confirmed in the Episcopal Church that he set his sights on an ideal but imaginary vision of pre-Reformation England as a guide not just to architecture but to the religious life.

Cram wrote the introduction to the 1913 edition of *Mont-Saint-Michel and Chartres*, the first public edition of a book first privately printed for Adams in 1904. Cram had obtained Henry Adams's permission to have the book published under the imprimatur of the American Institute Of Architects. Cram praised the book not only for its intrinsic interest but for "the cause it would so admirably serve."[2] (This would not have excited the almost aggressively disenchanted author.) Cram proclaimed the book a revelation: "all at once all the theology, philosophy, and mysticism, the politics, sociology, and economics, the romance, literature, and art of that greatest epoch of Christian civilization became fused in the alembic of an unique insight and precipitated by the dynamic force of a personal and distinguished style."[3]

With his usual mock modesty and disdain for the public—at least in old age—Adams gave "reluctant consent" to the general publication of the book, but, Cram added, "expressly stipulated that he should have no part or parcel in carrying out so mad a venture of faith—as he estimated the project of giving his book to the public."[4] I don't know whether Cram appreciated Adams's typical irony in using the word "faith"—about the public's finally getting a chance to acquire so learned a book about the Middle Ages though written in a "personal style." And this a book originally subtitled "A Study of Thirteenth-Century Unity." Unlike *The Education of Henry Adams*, the supposed companion piece to *Mont-Saint-Michel* as Adams's "autobiography," which was also first privately printed and then released for general publication after Adams's death in 1918, *Mont-Saint-Michel and Chartres* never won the Pulitzer Prize or had a steady life of its own in one format or another. In speaking of the "cause it could serve," Cram went beyond Adams's cryptic and probably arrogant conception

[2]Ralph Adams Cram, preface to *Mont-Saint-Michel and Chartres* (Boston, 1933), v.
[3]Ibid.
[4]Ibid., vi.

of the book's relation to himself. "Seven centuries dissolve and vanish away, being as they were not," Cram wrote in adoration of the book. "And it is well for us to have this experience."[5]

Apart from the desirable transformation it effects in preconceived and curiously erroneous superstitions as to one of the greatest eras in all history, it is vastly heartening and exhilarating.

If it gives new and not always flattering standards for the judgment of contemporary men and things, so does it establish new ideals, new goals for attainment. To live for one day in a world that built Chartres Cathedral, even if it makes the living in a world that creates the "Black Country" of England or an Iron City of America less a thing of joy and gladness than before, equally opens up the far prospect of another thirteenth century in the times that are to come and urges to ardent action towards its attainment.[6]

Cram's enormous and very stately Cathedral of Saint John the Divine, still unfinished and in its medieval fashion perhaps unfinishable, has not exactly inspired another thirteenth century on Amsterdam Avenue. The Episcopal Church of New York, once the largest landholder in Manhattan, is nowadays all too aware of the irony—a great medieval edifice amid so much poverty, ignorance and degradation. The cathedral is now as ecumenical as it is possible for an Episcopalian to be in torrentially multi-racial New York. Jewish intellectuals have been invited to address the faithful; there is a memorial right off the main door to Indian victims in Central America. Late in 1987 memorial services for James Baldwin filled the mighty church to the rafters. The tributes to Baldwin offered on that occasion by Toni Morrison, Amiri Baraka and other black artists were as bitter and "revolutionary" about American society as it is possible to be. In 1967 the current bishop of New York announced that the cathedral might never be completed but its staff would devote its energies to the poverty in the community surrounding it.

Perhaps Henry Adams would have relished the irony in all this, perhaps not. He had given up on American society except as a subject of inquiry and speculation. His own sense of social privilege was so pronounced that when he left Harvard for Washington in 1877, his friend Henry James made fun of him in the story "Pandora" as condescending even to presidents. Adams would not have seen the still colonial poverty of the Puerto Ricans surrounding Saint John the Divine any more than he saw

---

[5]Ibid., vii.
[6]Ibid., vii-viii.

the poor, diseased, beggars surrounding Chartres in the thirteenth century, or the Jews of Western Europe slaughtered to
the glory of God by the Crusaders as they made their way to the
Holy Land.

Adams was probably the wealthiest private scholar in the
United States, knew himself to possess absolutely first-class ability and resources. In his extraordinary freedom to travel and study
just as he liked, to say nothing of his contempt for the masses and
the political elites in his own country, he had become very grand
indeed. But did he write *Mont-Saint-Michel and Chartres* as the exercise in faith that the architect Cram found in *his* hopeful recon-
stitution of Gothic for the twentieth century? Did Adams write
even an inquiry *into* faith? To raise these questions is to involve
us in consideration of Adams's personal skepticism—something
quite different from his extraordinary historical intelligence and
insatiable curiosity, his narrative genius for absorbing himself in
a period and bringing it to life.

In the "Boston" chapter of the *Education* Adams, after noting
ironically that "nothing quieted doubt so completely as the mental calm of the Unitarian clergy," added "they proclaimed as their
merit that they insisted on no doctrine, but taught, or tried to
teach, the means of leading a virtuous, useful, unselfish life,
which they held to be sufficient for salvation. . . . Boston had
solved the universe, the problem was worked out."[7] Adams then
made a definitive statement about his own attitude toward religion that helps to explain his *cultural* rather than spiritual rapture
in turning to the Middle Ages:

Of all the conditions of his youth which afterwards puzzled the grown-
up man, this disappearance of religion puzzled him most . . . He went
through all the forms; but neither to him nor to his brothers or sisters
was religion real. Even the mild discipline of the Unitarian church was
so irksome that they all threw it off at the first possible moment, and
never afterwards entered a church. That the most powerful emotion of
man, next to the sexual, should disappear, might be a personal defect of
his own; but that the most intelligent society, led by the most intelligent
clergy, in the most moral conditions he ever knew, should have solved
all the problems of the universe so fully as to have quite ceased making
itself anxious about past or future, and should have persuaded itself
that all the problems which had convulsed human thought from earliest
recorded time, were not worth discussing, seemed to him the most cu-
rious phenomenon he had to account for in a long life.[8]

---

[7]Henry Adams, *Education*, 34.
[8]Ibid., 34.

The *Education*, in one of its many guises, even presents itself as the story of innocent ancestral certainty replaced, thanks to Lyell and Darwin, as exciting intellectual uncertainty. But it is clear from the whole drift of his book that Adams found this historic shift from religion to science utterly congenial. And as the last chapters of the book show, he became such an idolater of nineteenth-century positivism that he proclaimed the intellectual quest of his life to be the founding of history as science. Although he knew science only from secondary sources, he presumed in no very modest way to suggest that his own book was an example of science.

As for the Middle Ages! Adams was not a Pre-Raphaelite, not a seeker after lost paradises, not even an Anglo-Catholic like Cram. Saint John's Church in Washington, D.C., from which poor Marian Adams was buried, is right across the street from the Hay-Adams Hotel, the site of Adams's house. I am not aware that he ever attended it himself. Adams's professional interest in the medieval seems to have begun when as an assistant professor of history at Harvard he was asked to teach material intervening between the ancient and modern periods. Out of this experience came *Essays in Anglo-Saxon Law,* essays by his doctoral candidates that included his own "Anglo-Saxon Courts of Law." Adams was to train American medievalists like Henry Osborn Taylor and to inspire later ones like Frederick Bliss Luquiens and Albert Stansborough Cook.

This professional interest in the medieval accorded with a distinct trend in New England after the Civil War. Descendants of the rock-ribbed Puritans, impatient with the cultural limitations of their inheritance, were now passionate pilgrims to the Old World. As art and culture the Middle Ages beckoned to a country that owed its political faith to the Enlightenment. Medieval Europe, still on exhibition to those who had the means and the curiosity to visit it, gave relief, offered consolation, to those exceptional Americans who felt themselves deprived of ancient cathedrals and medieval legendry.

The Enlightenment in America had led the rationalist Thomas Jefferson and even the ancestrally devout John Quincy Adams to deride "monkish" habits, ways, and superstition as things of the past. Harvard was now becoming soft on the Middle Ages. There the study of Dante was to become an institution, first under Longfellow and his successor Lowell, in our century becoming an academic fixture under Charles Grandgent and Charles Singleton. Dante was to have a marked effect on Harvard poets, especially

T. S. Eliot. Earlier, Charles Eliot Norton helped to inaugurate a special interest in the Middle Ages with *Historical Studies of Church-Building in the Middle Ages* (1880). Norton was the son of the Unitarian divine Andrews Norton, among the first to attempt to prove the authenticity of the Bible from new critical sources. Charles Eliot Norton, who counseled Edith Wharton that "no great work of the imagination has ever been based on illicit passion,"[9] set the tone of medieval studies at Harvard through his belief in a strictly conceived but non-religious ethos, "derived from contemplation of the highest qualities of human nature."[10]

The tone of Harvard's Victorian medievalism was inevitably set by Cambridge's distance, in every sense, from thirteenth-century Italy. Norton commemorated his translation of *La Divina Commedia* with a poem of the same title that forlornly sighs in the gentlest possible tones over a world of religion and the fiercest passion closed to an American professor who was so far away from it all—and whose deepest belief was the inevitability of progress.

Henry Adams, first spending every summer in France, then for longer periods hiring attractive young women like Aileen Tone, who were expert in French, to find the words for the medieval chansons he loved to hear them sing, was right there in the *fin de siècle* when young Proust made a cult of Ruskin's medievalism and translated Ruskin's *The Bible of Amiens*. There was a marked nostalgia just then for the Middle Ages in France: some of it became politically aggressive with the neo-Catholic revival, directed against the leftist working class, the secularizing liberals, and the Jews during the Dreyfus "affaire." In England the aesthetic movement always suggested an imminent conversion to Rome, something the young high priest of the "beautiful," Oscar Wilde, accomplished only when he died in Paris in the most degraded circumstances.

The more upper-class American "pilgrims" returned to Europe, the more they were attracted to the church esthetically. The most irascible among them, like Henry Adams's eccentric brother Brooks, even began to dream in these increasingly strenuous times of a neo-medieval deliverance from what Henry Adams decried as "an economic civilization." But Henry knew too much history to believe in churchly deliverance. The more he saw of medieval France in that golden time when Americans of his class were the happy few to enjoy Europe for its monuments,

---

[9]Kermit Vanderbilt, *Charles Eliot Norton* (Cambridge, Mass., 1959), 178; Richard W. B. Lewis, *Edith Wharton* (London, 1975), 152.

[10]"Charles Eliot Norton." *Dictionary of American Biography* (1936), 13: 571.

landscapes, food and wine, the more his almost too supple imagination fastened on the thirteenth century as a drama of genius, taste, and aspiration.

In his American histories he had shown himself the most demanding student of social and economic facts. Nothing like that in the thirteenth century! No interest in *how* the Church spellbound and controlled the masses. No tiresome wars of tribute, no looting crusaders, no murders in the cathedral and disease raging outside it. Nothing but the glorious achievers of Chartres, Rheims, Amiens, Coutances; Norman architecture giving way to Gothic "flinging its passion against the sky"; the arts of sculpture and glass; the *Chanson de Roland*; courts of love; the *Summa Theologica* of Aquinas; the devotion of a period that found its ultimate sanction in the Virgin. She was the apotheosis of the feminine ideal to the age of chivalry. She now became that to the widower maddened by the suicide of his wife. He was forever seeking companionship from his nieces, from the young acolytes he made honorary "nieces," from his adored but inaccessible Elizabeth Cameron, the estranged wife of an American senator. The Virgin as the ultimate, perhaps composite, woman fitted into the historical dexterity of Henry Adams.

William James said in his tribute to *Mont-Saint-Michel* that it was characterized by "frolic power."[11] No Catholic apologist would have allowed himself such an ascent into intellectual fantasy as the widower and would-be lover of a senator's wife allowed himself in his portrait of the Virgin at Chartres. Abraham pictured about to sacrifice Isaac was to Adams "a compound horror of masculine stupidity and brutality."[12] But as for the Virgin—

She was still a woman, who loved grace, beauty, ornament—her toilette, robes, jewels;—who considered the arrangements of her palace with attention, and liked both light and color; who kept a keen eye on her Court, and exacted prompt and willing obedience from king and archbishops as from beggars and drunken priests. She protected her friends and punished her enemies. She required space, beyond what was known in the Courts of Kings, because she was liable at all times to have ten thousand people begging her for favors—mostly inconsistent with law—and deaf to refusal. She was extremely sensitive to neglect, to disagreeable impressions, to want of intelligence in her surroundings. She was the greatest artist, as she was the greatest philosopher and musician and theologist, that ever lived on earth, except her Son, Who, at

---

[11]Quoted in Ernest Samuels, *Henry Adams: The Major Phase* (Cambridge, Mass., 1964), 308.
[12]Henry Adams, *Mont-Saint-Michel and Chartres* (Boston, 1933), 82.

Chartres, is still an Infant under her guardianship. Her taste was infallible; her sentence eternally final.[13]

If this was plainly infatuation—with a symbol—the weight of so much symbolism was what Adams respected as culture. The Virgin by her authority enforced this culture into a unity forever dazzling later centuries. The demon of unity drove Adams in his autobiography to restore some unity to a life divided by Marian's death and, equally, to a squalid "economic civilization." The world was flying apart. Unity was what modern civilization, with his own country in the perilous lead, found itself gasping for as faith dissolved in every sphere. Faith as such was not the issue, and to Adams it was clearly not recoverable. Whatever he wrote of religion, Western and Oriental, shows that he approached it as an anthropologist, a comparative religionist. Nor did he believe, with Ruskin and Proust, that the pursuit of beauty alone could lead to intellectual salvation.

What fascinated this descendant of "Puritans and Patriots," as he proudly styled himself, this heir of zealous Calvinists who had built first a new world for rebels against ecclesiastical orthodoxy, then had written for a new country a constitution established on philosophic principles—was mind, achievement, talent, genius, the lights of superior intellect, the victories of spirit. Adams, the historian of minds in *Mont-Saint-Michel*, is always representing in everything he studied and observed the beauty of intelligence, which alone rises above the fragmentation and dissolution of earthly experience. Adams was not one to bow to the Cross. He may never have read Nietzsche on the Death of God, but he was as cheerful on the subject as Nietzsche counseled modern man to be. But for him there was nothing like "mind," which he liked to picture as a meteor flashing through space.

It is this, where Adams closes his book on the stupendous achievement of Saint Thomas Aquinas, that comes out in the triumph of Thomas's mind *over* his system, over the church his system helped to buttress. The mind naturally classifies and positions its thoughts, and so unites. The mind labors in a climate of unity whether it wants to or not. And calls that unity whatever it will. In the thirteenth century, "God"; in the age of entropy, chance, random occurrences, systematized meaninglessness, its name for Adams was "chaos." But men are driven to seek unity, in letter, name, symbol, by the very nature of the

---

[13]Ibid., 88.

mind. So what a tragedy for culture if the civilization surrounding mind is without form or plan or belief in anything except material advancement! This can lead thoughtful men back to the Middle Ages. To recover even the conscious wish for unity can drive a man to write about the thirteenth century at the beginning of the twentieth.

It is the grip of time, time recovered, that Adams shared with Proust when the great cathedrals became an image less of eternity than of human genius. Art had become the new religion for Proust, not for Adams. At the end of his book he was still pretending that all this was just what an American tourist could bring back from a heavenly summer in France.

About Saint Thomas's theology we need not greatly disturb ourselves; it can matter now not much, whether he put more pantheism than the law allowed or more materialism than Duns Scotus approved—or less of either—into his universe, since the Church is still on the spot, responsible for its own doctrines; but his architecture is another matter.[14]

---

[14]Ibid., 374.

HENRY ADAMS'S ANTHROPOLOGICAL VISION AS AMERICAN IDENTITY

Eugenia Kaledin

I.

The mind of Henry Adams, shaped as it was by eighteenth-century political theory and nineteenth-century social reality, astonishes us today with its twentieth-century anthropological dimension. Adams's capacity both to look beyond his white New England upbringing for new ideas of culture and to consider women seriously as more than just subsidiary to men—as "force" or gender culture—clearly foreshadows the revisionist history that has emerged in America since the 1960s. In 1988 the American Studies Association annual meeting called itself: "Creativity in Difference: The Cultures of Gender, Race, Ethnicity and Class." If one part of Henry Adams might have been appalled by the crudities of such a scholarly meeting at the Fontainebleau Hotel in Miami Beach, another part would, I believe, also have been moved by the continuing search among younger scholars for a richer American identity.

"Ever Yr. H. Pocahontas Adams," Henry signed himself playfully in an 1869 letter to his English friend, Charles Milnes Gaskell. The letter, as was habitual in Henry Adams's correspondence, contrasted the American scene with Gaskell's reports of royal scandal. In Washington, insisted Adams, "we are vulgar but correct." And he went on to describe his own recent work as a critical journalist in the capital, "held up solely by social position and a sharp tongue."[1] The "autobiography" he wrote in all his letters to Gaskell also included family details, for the two had been intimate since Henry's Civil War years spent in London as secretary to his ambassador father. Gaskell remained a friend with whom Henry might continue to share "mild hope and consolation from literature and art and that society where

---

[1]J. C. Levenson, et al., eds.; *The Letters of Henry Adams*, 3, 1886-1892, (Cambridge, Mass., 1982), 56, 54.

our calmness is not ruffled by obnoxious people."[2] The American vulgarity Henry described was never easy for an Adams to live with or to record. Although he could express his feelings freely to a close friend like Gaskell, he would not, he added, send his more critical writings to British "America-phobists" to encourage their contempt for his flawed country. "H. Pocahontas" concluded this lengthy epistle written over several days with an account of his first visit to President and Mrs. Grant, reminding readers of the Henry James story "Pandora," thought to describe the Adamses' idea of entertaining the president as doing something really vulgar. Henry wrote that Mrs. Grant "squinted like an isosceles triangle," but he added "she is not much more vulgar than some duchesses." With easy arrogance the youthful descendant of two presidents concluded: "I flatter myself it was I who showed them [the Grants] how they ought to behave. One feels such an irresistible desire, as you know, to tell this kind of individual to put themselves at their ease and talk just as though they were at home."[3]

Although young Henry's patronizing tone may well discourage the modern reader who recognizes the superficiality of many of his complaints, the role Adams had chosen for himself as culture critic remains a serious one. The ongoing dilemmas of the honest intellectual committed to democracy are real. The "vulgar," the "obnoxious," and more chillingly, "the immoral" citizens running the government his forefathers had helped shape, daily challenged Henry's faith in his country—as corrupt leaders continue to trouble political idealists. And although many years later Henry Adams would finish his own nine-volume history of the United States with the statement that American destiny had to be defined in terms of "the people alone," rather than in terms of "wars" or "heroes," his personal experiences with "the people alone" more often than not ended in disappointment.[4] Trying to come to terms with his democratic identity, I believe, drove Henry Adams to explore other cultures with a seriousness that may well be undervalued in most appraisals of his American self.

Henry always wanted to extend his Harvard training. He yearned, he once wrote, to escape " 'Culture' with a capital C" in order to "come in contact with the wider life I have always found so much more to my taste." In turning away from that academic

[2]Ibid., 56.

[3]Ibid., 56. See also Henry James, "Pandora," *The Complete Tales of Henry James*, 5 (Philadelphia, 1963).

[4]Henry Adams, *History of the United States of America*, 9 (New York, 1889-1991): 224.

culture that represented "all the very latest European fashions,"[5] he also became one of the first American historians to value an anthropological dimension in interpreting reality. To be sure, Henry Adams did not in any historical sense "go native" or deliberately champion a less inhibited value system in the manner of modern writers like D. H. Lawrence. As far as I can tell he did not consciously perceive any connection between the ethnic hordes he saw taking over his world and the study of heathen cultures[6] that continued to fascinate him. But in a transcendental way—perhaps quite clearly Emersonian (like his rejection of European culture)—he recognized the power of the unifying force in cultures that differed entirely from his limited Anglo-Saxon background. Just two years before he wrote his Pocahontas letter he had published an article on John Smith's experiences in Virginia, based on research done in England during our Civil War—perhaps Adams's oblique way to stress his patriotism as he debunked one of the heroes of the South.

"Captaine John Smith: Sometime Governour in Virginia and Admirall of New England," appeared in 1867 in *The North American Review*. With painstaking accuracy and his usual literary grace Henry Adams demonstrated the discrepancies between the two versions of Smith's American adventures. In the earlier version, "the safer authority for historians to follow (an established law of historical criticism)," Adams noted that the Indian princess did not appear as Smith's savior but he commented that "the behavior of the Indians toward Smith was more humane than he would have received at the hands of civilized peoples."[7] Our scientific historian could not entertain the idea that the first version might have been designed to emphasize Smith's European self-sufficiency. Pocahontas, nevertheless, as Adams described the known details of her life remained entirely charming. Adams ferreted out every known reference to Powhatan's daughter; he shows her cartwheeling about in a scanty leaf skirt, and he records her conversion to Christianity and her subsequent marriage—not to John Smith but to John Rolfe. Pocahontas's voyage to England to meet the king and queen, Adams asserted, made her "the most conspicuous figure in Virginia." And finally her early death abroad as a young mother gave Adams the chance to

---

[5]*Letters*, 2 (1868-1885), 239.

[6]See Werner Sollers, "Literature and Ethnicity," *Harvard Encyclopedia of American Ethnic Groups*, Stephan Thernstrom et al., eds. (Cambridge, Mass., 1980), for a useful discussion of the root connections of ethnic and heathen.

[7]Henry Adams, *Historical Essays*, (New York, 1891), 54.

demonstrate a sympathy for Native American royalty never accorded the common soldier of fortune John Smith.[8]

Adams acknowledged that the Pocahontas legend even then was familiar to every schoolboy and that Virginia families of "the highest claim to merit trace their descent from the Emperor's daughter that saved the life of Captain John Smith." Had there been no "romantic incidents" in Pocahontas's life, Adams argued, they were likely to be invented. Smith, whose character "was always a matter of doubt," published the second version of his history in 1624 *after* all the main characters were dead; he had embellished his original account because Pocahontas appealed so strongly to "the popular imagination attracted by a wild and vigorous picture of savage life." Yet John Smith himself died a failure, Adams concluded with some satisfaction. What succeeded was the established "credulity" that left the story "unquestioned almost to the present day"—the myth that no amount of scientific evidence could dispel—"ever perpetuated in its retelling." "The growth of a legend," Adams wisely conceded, may well be as "interesting as the question of its truth."[9]

The Pocahontas story, a classical example of the folklore of the vulgar adventurer rescued by the exotic patrician, is also one of our rare American myths. That Henry Adams still in his twenties picked the legend for historical enquiry shows us how complex and original he could be. His efforts to become a scientific historian drove him ever to confront realities for which he could find no answers in libraries. Anticipating a vision of the modern anthropologist by Clifford Geertz, Adams began to reach beyond a "laws-and-instances ideal of explanation toward a cases-and-interpretations one, looking less for the sort of thing that connects planets and pendulums and more for the sort that connects chrysanthemums and swords."[10] If not yet ready to focus on symbol as an organizing force in history Adams nonetheless began to consider social patterns that related as much to intuition as to quantities of fact. In his decision to debunk John Smith, Henry Adams reminds the twentieth-century reader just how pervasive the myth of the powerful Indian princess has been in American culture. Pocahontas's legend extends beyond the folklore of royal rescuer to every level of American consciousness in hundreds of

---

[8]Ibid., 56, 77.

[9]Ibid., 76, 77, 62.

[10]Clifford Geertz, "Blurred Genres: The Refiguration of Social Thought," *American Scholar*, 49 (Spring 1980), 165.

versions: from comic books and cigar store Indians and popular music to the writings of Hart Crane, Vachel Lindsay, and John Barth. And if Pocahontas's conversion to Christianity now also suggests disloyalty to her family and to her tribal culture, the story of her life continues to emphasize the possibility of the mixture of race and culture through marriage that has become as real to modern society as the laws against miscegenation were to the past.[11] The extreme adaptability necessary for survival for all new Americans in a new land among new people continues to demand reinforcement in our mythology at every intellectual level. The tale of Pocahontas also suggests an important additional myth: that it was possible for the Native American, after all, to adjust easily to European ways. Not only did Pocahontas's personal integrity manage to save the "civilized" Englishman from the "savages" who were her people but she also demonstrated her own capacity for conversion to a "superior" civilization. She had herself baptized "Rebecca," suggesting the total renunciation of former culture experienced by all immigrants for a time at least in their acceptance of this new world.

"No American needs to learn that Pocahontas is the most romantic character in the history of his country,"[12] Adams asserted. In reminding readers of *The North American Review* of the importance of the Indian princess, symbol of native fertility and vigor, "cartwheeling through our veins and down the generations,"[13] Henry Adams first hit upon the idea of force that was more than fact. The power that represented salvation through Pocahontas— the female—demonstrated a dimension of reality that would much later find definition in his imagination of the Virgin of Chartres. When Henry jokingly signed his letter to Gaskell, "H. Pocahontas," he proudly identified himself—as in his novels— not with a hero but with a heroine. He understood the integrity of the woman—of the American royalty—who was also an outsider and therefore intellectually free to be critical.

As a journalist Henry Adams carefully honed his critical intelligence; he began to feel that there would always be some Americans who would heed his opinions: "I get along better on my native heath with tomahawk and feathers than I did in sword and

---

[11]See Mary V. Dearborn, *Pocahontas's Daughters: Gender and Ethnicity in American Culture* (New York, 1986), for a recent examination of this idea.

[12]"Captaine John Smith," 56.

[13]Philip Young, "The Mother of Us All: Pocahontas Reconsidered," *Kenyon Review*, 4 (Summer 1962), 407.

breeches at Buckingham Palace,"[14] he would write his English
friend again, suggesting also that he was always prepared to
fight. The eighteenth-century figure Adams would later label
himself was ever more committed to the earlier century's dream
of the noble savage than to his own century's expansionist ration-
ales for the Indians' extinction. In the seven years he was editor
of *The North American Review* (1870-1877) Henry Adams would
continue to distinguish himself from those more proper Bosto-
nians who "knelt in self-abasement before the majesty of English
standards."[15] He tried to record details about the Native American cultures he saw on the brink of being wiped out; and he included essays on a variety of other societies in order to expand
the consciousness of the parochial American. As an editor Adams
established himself as an example of the anthropological thinker
defined by Ruth Benedict, "interested in human behavior, not as
it is shaped by one tradition" but "interested in the great gamut
of custom that is found in various cultures." Like Benedict too,
Adams wanted "to understand the way in which these cultures
change and differentiate" particularly in order to understand
how environments "shape the individual."[16] Although the evo-
lutionary racism that was characteristic of many nineteenth-
century attitudes toward other societies appears occasionally in
the work of Adams's reviewers, more often we find signs of a
genuine cultural relativism, an open-mindedness concerned
much more with cultural variety than with white supremacy.
American readers of *The North American Review* would feel that
exotic cultures were being studied in terms of the people who
created them, not, as George Stocking has suggested of contemporary British ethnologists, simply "to cast light on the processes
by which the ape had developed into the British gentleman."[17]

To Lewis Henry Morgan, an authority on the social structure of
ancient societies, a truly distinguished amateur anthropologist
and frequent contributor to the *Review*, Henry wrote:

The portion relating to our Indians interests me greatly and fills a
gap. . . . *It must be the foundation of all future work in American Historical*

---

[14]*Letters*, 5.1: 2; See also *Letters* 5.2: "I want to revert to the ancestral type and in this
country it is not the politician; it is the Mexican Indian who knows life" (421). "We are
getting our blankets, tomahawks, feathers and war paint out, to show how effective our
couleur locale may be" (356).
[15]*The Education of Henry Adams* (hereafter *EHA*), ed. with introd. and notes by Ernest and
Jayne Samuels (Boston, 1974), 312.
[16]Ruth Benedict, *Patterns of Culture* (Boston, 1934, 1959), 1, 2.
[17]George W. Stocking, Jr., *Victorian Anthropology* (New York, 1987), 185.

science and I hope that no time will be lost in pressing the same class of inquiries among the existing tribes of Indians which have come least in contact with civilisation. (Italics mine)

Twentieth-century readers may well note that it has taken another hundred years for American historians to recognize as Adams did in 1877, that such research should be included in the foundations of *all* American history. Committed to scientific inquiry into the "laws and usages" of the remaining Indian tribes, Henry concluded with urgency that much material "still in existence will not last much longer."[18]

To Henry Adams the Native Americans—curiously like the immigrant individuals spreading out over their lands—seemed to begin life without historical precedent. He recognized how important it was to establish Native American histories, to attempt to trace their ancestral roots. Although not prepared to accept Margaret Mead's definition of Americans as people who have substituted space for time, he was beginning to understand that people in this new world had to build a new identity based "on their growing sense of what men of all races and creeds . . . peasants, savages, princes, or statesmen might 'bring forth upon this continent.' "[19] Documenting Native American achievements, Adams thought, would help his contemporaries better to deal with Indian customs. Morgan's *League of the Iroquois*, he knew, had done much to clarify the laws and complex government of the New York tribes. Adams solicited similar materials from other men who were knowledgeable about the West. From John Wesley Powell he requested a map of all extant Indian tribes with population figures. He was pleased to include a review of Raphael Pumpelly's *Across America and Asia: Notes of a Five Years' Journey Around the World and of Residence in Arizona, China and Japan*. That Arizona was considered as remote as China tells us much about the limited worlds of contemporary readers. Included from Pumpelly was the valuable discovery that "barbarity on the part of the Red men is due chiefly to the injustice and duplicity of the whites."[20]

Adams remained challenged by the intellectual possibility that all cultures repeated the same ethnic patterns. But making social

---

[18]*Letters*, 2: 311. See also: James H. Merrell, "Some Thoughts on Colonial Historians and American Indians," *The William and Mary Quarterly*, 5.46 (January 1989): 94–119.

[19]*The Golden Age of American Anthropology*, ed. with introd. and notes by Margaret Mead and Ruth L. Bunzel (New York, 1960), 2.

[20]*North American Review* (hereafter *NAR*), 116: 225.

systems out of great variety was never easy. As Henry Adams asked Lewis Morgan, "Are we to consider our Indians as in the first stage of social development . . . or in the second or third?" Whatever would become established fact did not seem to matter as much as the pragmatic clarification: "Our American ethnology is destined to change the fashionable European theories of history to no small extent."[21] Francis Parkman was the reviewer Adams chose to write on Hubert Howe Bancroft's work on *The Native Races of the Pacific States*, in two volumes: "The Wild Tribes" and "The Civilized." Yet no strong political views on the Native American emerged. An unsigned review of Francis Amasa Walker's *The Indian Question* described the Indians as a semi-civilized "obstacle to progress"; but the reviewer concluded with a plea for "justice and mercy to a race which has been impoverished that we might be made richer."[22] It was possible for a thoughtful reader to begin to wonder about the price Americans paid for their own "civilization."

Under Adams's editorship comparative religion and mythology also found voice in *The North American Review*. Cross-cultural studies like Anna Leonowen's accounts of her life in Siam: *The English Governess at the Siamese Court* and *The Romance of the Harem* were treated respectfully next to erudite linguistic studies and essays on "The Germanic World of the Gods" and "Songs of the Russian People."

The multiplicity that Henry Adams would come to mistrust as characteristic of the modern world was also a profound part of his free personality; *E Pluribus Unum*, the motto John Adams had helped to choose to represent the complexity of the newly United States, remained deeply rooted in his great-grandson's consciousness of America. On a political level Henry Adams continued to explore how leaders emerged in those cultures lacking Anglo-Saxon legal traditions. As early as 1870, *The North American Review* had published an article on the Chinese Civil Service exams. Echoing the fears he had expressed about democracy to Gaskell, Adams also wrote to John G. Palfrey: "The great problem of every system of government has been to place administration and legislation in the hands of the best men . . . an idea that in America, naturally clashes with our other fundamental principle that one man is as good as another." As Adams saw himself playing the role of the significant outsider, the culture critic rather

---

[21]*Letters*, 2: 266, 271.
[22]*NAR*, 116: 388.

than the policy maker, he felt free to write of Washington: "The more I see of official life here, the less I am inclined to want to enter it."[23] Concern for placing government in the hands of "the best men," as Abigail Adams might well have remarked, also failed to consider the powerful roles so often played by women in other societies. Henry Adams himself had defined their strength in Native American culture when he made us realize that Pocahontas remained more significant than the great chief, Powhatan, her father.

In 1872 Henry had married Marian (Clover) Hooper, an unusually bright, financially independent woman whose family included a Transcendental poet as well as a number of reformers and free-thinkers. Her grandfather, William Sturgis, once boasted to fellow legislators who addressed him in Latin that although he did not know the Roman language he knew well the dialects of the Northwest Indian. Clover's aunt, Caroline Sturgis, was the choice of feminist Margaret Fuller to rear her child if anything happened to her in revolutionary Italy. Also a close friend of Waldo Emerson's, Caroline (Carrie) urged the Concord philosopher in England in 1872 to convey her gratitude to John Stuart Mill: "I should like to thank John Stuart Mill for being just & understanding that women are slaves still politically—& therefore socially—& for so nobly protesting against the injustice shown them."[24] Except for a few remarks about Henry's friend Francis Parkman, who was outspoken against women's rights, Clover kept quiet about women's issues after her marriage to Henry, but it is clear that her upbringing fostered respect for women's capabilities outside the home.

Clover's father, also an unusual man, not only cut back on his practice as an ophthalmologist to raise his children after his wife's early death, but also regularly volunteered his services in hospitals for the mentally ill. Among the Hoopers Henry Adams would discover a dimension of social service that lay outside his own family's adherence to diplomacy and law; the powers demonstrated by Clover's relatives might well have reinforced his own growing skepticism of the world of politics. And Adams was reminded once again and more intimately of the remarkable force of women who were—as he himself would choose symbolically to become—outsiders. When he decided four years after his

---

[23]*Letters*, 2: 19.

[24]Quoted in Eugenia Kaledin, *The Education of Mrs. Henry Adams* (Philadelphia, 1982), 133. Other examples of Clover's family's commitment to women are cited throughout this text.

marriage to explore the meaning of "Women's Rights in History" for a lecture at the Lowell Institute in 1876, Henry Adams brought an enriched awareness to his efforts to look beyond Pocahontas into pre-history.

Like his good friend Henry James, Adams was fascinated by the social energies implicit in women's lives. If he was not yet ready to analyze the vigor and tragedy of the women in his own world, he was at least ready to explore their historical origins. The Lowell Institute lecture distinguishes Henry as one of our first "Gender Historians." Not concerned with the "separate spheres" thesis, designed to keep women in the home, that defined most nineteenth-century attitudes toward women, Adams was interested—as feminist deconstructionists would be today—in looking at the way women's presence gave a richer "meaning to the organization and perception of historical knowledge."[25] Whether at this stage Henry Adams knew the work of Lydia Maria Child, a Transcendental contemporary of Clover's mother who published, in 1835, *The History of the Condition of Women in Various Ages and Nations,* is uncertain; perhaps he would have placed her among the female story tellers, the women historians he later disdained. But like Child, Adams was more attentive to the strong women who survived than to the women who were victims. His goal would seem to match exactly Natalie Zemon Davis's recent justification of gender studies: "to discover the range in sex roles and in sexual symbolism in different societies and periods, to find out what meaning they had and how they functioned in the social order or to promote its change."[26] Adams was eager to expand the knowledge of women's powers in societies that had no connections with British institutions. To Lewis Morgan he wrote again requesting more information about divorce among Native Americans: "I see you state that their marriage permitted separation at will of either party; . . . if this can be proved I should be glad to know the facts."[27]

Naturally, Adams's reflections on women related to his ongoing concerns about the nature of power. How early societies chose their leaders was still a lively topic for speculation. It seemed clear that women in a number of "primitive" societies not only had rights but also wielded greater influence than the

---

[25]Joan Wallach Scott, "Gender: A Useful Category of Historical Analysis," *American Historical Review,* 91 (December 1986), 1055.

[26]Natalie Zemon Davis, "Women's History in Transition: The European Case," *Feminist Studies,* 3 (Spring 1976), 90. See also "What is Women's History?" *History Today* (June 1985): 35-40.

[27]*Letters,* 2: 271.

nineteenth-century male wanted to imagine. Many of Adams's contemporaries not only accepted women's biological inferiority, but believed as well that her pre-historical role had been one of perpetual slavery. Once again Adams relished debunking what seemed far-fetched to him.

That Henry Adams, whose personal life abounds in records of admiration for many women, should have set out to explore women's cultural history is no surprise to any who know him well: "The position of women—or Woman if you prefer—in an archaic society—has always interested me,"[28] he wrote a niece many years later from Samoa. Again long before modern anthropologists would find Samoan culture a fruitful source of comparison with the sexual mores of the United States, Henry Adams was there exploring the world of "old gold" women his friend the geologist Clarence King admired so intensely. Adams prided himself always on his originality and his capacity to make up his own mind on every sort of popular issue. As editor of *The North American Review* he included an unsympathetic review of Dr. Edward Clarke's notorious 1873 book on women's biological incapacity to learn: *Sex in Education*. The reviewer, quite possibly Adams himself, made it clear that nothing in his personal experience reinforced Clarke's assertions that women had smaller brains or that their monthly weakness made it impossible for them to share the rigors of college education.[29] Included in 1875 again was a review of Clarke's second book, *The Building of a Brain*, another attempt to deny women access to men's opportunities. It seems certain to me that Henry Adams would have applauded the final rebuttal: "There are plenty of tolerably healthy women among us, and these not merely Indians, working women and servants, but such as can and do move with the foremost in their respected spheres."[30]

Adams knew well that women's "improved" nineteenth-century status could be far from liberating for all classes of

---

[28]*Letters*, 3: 324.

[29]Edward Chalfant in his edition of Henry Adams's *Sketches for the North American Review* (Hamden, 1986), 228-232, argues elegantly that Henry Adams did not write either of these reviews. I regret that the circumstantial evidence does not convince me. Although past biographers have argued that such an interest on Adams's part was "unlikely," I would argue that the opposite is true. No passages are more poignant in his writings than those on the wasted brilliance of his sister Louisa, or his appreciation of his unhappy mother's intellect. His close association with the Gurneys who were active pioneers in establishing Radcliffe College is undeniable. Many of his wife's letters also testify to her happiness when she was helping Henry with his intellectual labors. To deny Henry Adams this sensitivity to women's need for serious education is to diminish him. See *The Education of Mrs. Henry Adams*.

[30]*NAR*, 120: 188.

contemporary women. But when he started to examine the lives
of prehistoric women for his lecture (later published as "Primitive
Rights of Women"), he would probably not have designed his
talk to contrast archaic conventions with current institutional re-
straints. With characteristic circumspection, however, Adams
pointed out that the "primitive" or "communistic" stage of society offered women opportunities for political power. He repeated
his belief in the good fortune of American students' not having to
depend on "mere Historical theory." They could study "the entire race of American Indians from Behring's Straits to the Straits
of Magellan" to witness still "the stage of communism."[31] Although the tribes bound to matrilinear connections must have
struck Henry at the time as inferior to those in Central America
where "fathers" controlled heredity conditions, Adams's own
mind remained open as he speculated on the history of relations
between the sexes. It would still be many years before he could
write that he had abandoned the society of his fathers, whose political predicaments he had also taken pains to explore in nine
volumes of scrupulously written history: or to insist as a "general
law of experience—no woman had ever driven him wrong; no
man had ever driven him right."[32]

The lecture on the early rights of women flows easily from a
discussion of women's powers among Native Americans back to
their treatment in ancient Egypt. No one could enter an Egyptian
museum (as he and Clover must have done on their honeymoon)
"without seeing the weakness of any theory which assigns to
Egyptian women, even in extreme antiquity, the position of
slaves." Royalty invariably sit side by side as equals. Here too,
Adams remarks "the female line of descent was followed regularly if not invariably among Egyptians as among American
Indians."[33] Although burdened with the values of his forefathers
Henry nonetheless appeared capable of appreciating other ap-
proaches to reality. His open-mindedness, reflecting the self he
would later label "failure," enabled him, as Raymond Williams
has put it, to unlearn "the inherent dominant mode."[34] In scru-
tinizing the rights of primitive women, Adams forced himself to
consider their valor and to wonder at the source of the submissive
role women all too frequently played in the contemporary world.
"The rise of Christianity," he finally concluded, "marked the

---

[31]"Primitive Rights of Women," *Historical Essays*, 7.
[32]*EHA*, 85.
[33]"Primitive Rights," 12.
[34]Quoted in Edward Said, *Orientalism* (New York, 1979), 28.

diminution of women's social and legal rights." The idea of "obedience to Bishop and to husband tended to depress the women's civil rights" and to make them "more dependent on the church for consolation and protection."[35]

With the "willing cooperation" of men, Adams continued, the Church raised up "the modern type of Griselda,—the meek and patient, the silent and tender sufferer, the pale reflection of the Mater Dolorosa, submissive to every torture that her husband could invent, but more submissive to the church than to her husband." For after all, the Kingdom of Heaven was hers. At this stage of his life, Adams asserted that "Mariolatry, the worship of the Virgin Mother—proved how strongly human nature revolted" against the actual degradation of women; the unity fostered by her spiritual force was not yet important to him. But it would be hard to argue indeed that Henry Adams ever admired any image of a submissive woman. The characters who stand out in this lecture are like the woman he married, independent thinkers. Hallgerda and Penelope also like Pocahontas assert their individuality as much as possible within the framework of their archaic societies—much as Clover Adams attempted to do within the tradition of free-thinking women that shaped her own "proud, self-confident, vindictive background."[36]

After Clover's suicide in 1885, Henry Adams, perhaps eager to explore cultures that had influenced her world more than his own, would turn to the East. Many Americans have looked to Asia for answers to Western dilemmas. And many have also sought in exotic societies the vitality they could not appreciate in the immigrant presence at home.

II.

Nirvana was out of season, a reporter insisted as Henry Adams and John La Farge set out together on the first of two long trips to the Orient, in the summer of 1886. Why would Henry Adams, always sea-sick, make such pilgrimages to the East, generously subsidizing his traveling companion's expenses? What did this son of Anglo-Saxon Boston hope to find beyond the Pacific that was lacking on Beacon Hill and missing in Washington?[37]

After Clover took her life Henry tried to open his mind more to the possibility that the Adams family's political answers were not

---

[35]"Primitive Rights," 36, 37.
[36]Ibid., 15, 38. See also chaps. 2, 3, and 5 in *The Education of Mrs. HA.*
[37]*Letters*, 3: 12.

the only reality. The many letters he received after her death helped him realize that he was not simply a member of an elite group of similar "hearts," but a part of a "vast fraternity" of the "Hearts that Ache."[38] Before turning eastward the second time in 1890, he commissioned Augustus Saint-Gaudens—whose works Clover had greatly admired—to begin designing a memorial monument for them both, a work of art that would liberate the mind of the observer to meditate rather than bind it to any one system of beliefs. If organized Christianity, as Henry knew it in the nineteenth century and tried to demonstrate in his novel *Esther*, provided little comfort to the independent spirit, perhaps other cultures might offer spiritual solace not found in familiar Western ritual. In Asia, Henry Adams could also explore those international experiences that were entirely foreign to his European-Adams background. Clover's family with its Transcendental connections and its China trade wealth had always made much of their oriental connections. Her cousin Sturgis Bigelow actually became a Buddhist. And in one letter Clover's mother, the poet, insisted that she was much more like the Chinese than like the New England "Busy Bee." The *Dial*, the voice of Transcendental thinking, had published her poetry along with *Ethnical Scriptures: Selections from Oriental Books*. Emerson, not admired by any Adams, but called by Clover's sister, "the Apostle of their youth,"[39] would write in his Journals with certainty: "Buddhist is a Transcendentalist."[40] After Clover's death Henry, identifying more with his wife than with his father, opened his mind more charitably to Emersonian thinking. He seemed to accept in theory at least, the Concord sage's dictum that "Oriental largeness" was a remedy for the "self-conceited modish life made up of trifles clinging to corporeal civilization, hating ideas."[41]

"Mine Asia," Emerson had called his wife, Lidian, suggesting as well that Asia might also represent the feminine world of mystery that complemented the male world of daily action: that force or power continued to haunt Henry Adams.[42]

Yet the Nirvana that Adams and La Farge sought in Japan was indeed out of season. Henry's letters record many more complaints about Japan than satisfactions: evil smells, badly built

---

[38]Ibid., 5.

[39]Quoted in *Educat. of Mrs. HA*, 31.

[40]RWE *Journals*, 5.7, quoted in Frederic I. Carpenter, *Emerson and Asia* (Cambridge, Mass., 1930), 148.

[41]"English Traits," *The Complete Works of Ralph Waldo Emerson* (Boston, 1903-1904), 5: 258.

[42]Carpenter, chap. 2, 27–39.

women, childish people. "The only solemn fact of life" he wrote his friend John Hay, "is the tea ceremony."[43] While in Japan he made a point of visiting Clover's cousin, William Sturgis Bigelow, who joined a Buddhist monastery there, and Ernest Fenollosa who had also become part of a Buddhist sect; yet the discipline these men found in accepting the rigid cultural codes of an Eastern religion was not a part of Henry Adams's needs.

He continued to relish the intellectual freedom that caused him so many dilemmas. With characteristic wit he wrote John Hay again: "I was myself a Buddhist when I left America, but he [Fenollosa] has converted me to Calvinism with leanings toward the Methodist." La Farge, his artistic mentor, did manage to dislodge some of Henry's prejudices by teaching him to value the harmony of nature and culture the Japanese sometimes achieved. By the end of the summer Adams wrote: "Buddhist contemplation of the infinite seems the only natural mode of life."[44] But sometimes he was simply reminded of the great natural beauty of America. In one bathhouse where he came upon a group of naked men, women and children, he fancied he had at last found "a thousand year old scene." And by October 1886 after his return to the United States, Adams's restlessness reappeared: "China is the only mystery left to penetrate. . . . As soon as I can get rid of history and the present I mean to start for China and stay there." Japan, after all, he concluded, was "only a sort of antechamber to China."[45]

Confronting America, but still yearning, Henry Adams wrote to his old friend Gaskell: "Society is getting new tastes and history of the old school has not many years to live." And to another British friend, Robert Cunliffe: "Japan gave me so much to think about that I am eager to start again, not for Japan but for China."[46] The Buddhism his scientific self had earlier rejected on the scene in 1886, had by 1888 become a real part of his personal search for the infinite. Writing of his cemetery monument in the one undestroyed fragment of his diary that remains, Henry noted that with La Farge and Saint-Gaudens he "made another step in advance towards my Buddha grave." Adams had lent the sculptor photographs of Chinese statues of Buddha for inspiration. A figure Saint-Gaudens would imagine as "sexless and passionless," expressing the philosophic calm so rare in active Western life,

---

[43]*Letters*, 3: 19.
[44]Ibid., 24, 29.
[45]Ibid., 33, 44.
[46]Ibid., 49; 52-53.

became the focus of the sculptor's energies. By September 1888 Adams did not hesitate to record also that he was equally concerned about the setting; he noted the contract he had made with Stanford White "for stonework of Buddha monument at Rock Creek," and by December he recorded again with satisfaction that Saint-Gaudens had "begun the Buddha."[47]

Henry Adams's Diary mentions as well his intention to learn a thousand Chinese characters thoroughly. "Studying Chinese," he had written John Hay, "stills most complaints." He would return to East Asia as soon as he concluded his nine-volume history of the United States in which, as he told Hay:

> . . . all my wicked villains will be duly rewarded with presidencies and the plunder of the innocent; all my models of usefulness and intelligence will be fitly punished, and deprived of office and honors; all my stupid people including readers, will be put to sleep for a thousand years.

Small wonder that Adams wrote in his diary on the very same day: "I am nearly Buddha."[48]

Fearing that the Chinese exclusion bill might well bring about retaliatory measures that would keep him out of China, he also wrote Gaskell to suggest that his desire to explore Eastern culture might well compensate for his exasperation with the immigrants who kept pouring into America: "The Chinaman takes the place of the ubiquitous Irishman, politics and all." He added: "Both are rather a bore; but the Chinaman bores one in a new way."[49] Anyone who reads much Henry Adams grows accustomed to such statements which are not easy to interpret but show clearly that he remains hostilely aware of the presence of "outsiders." The complex philosophical vision he had begun to honor in Confucius and Lao-Tse harmonized with his own reluctance to expose his vulnerability, but he never got to China to test its reality in practice; the Chinese again closed their doors. When he set out for Asia in 1891, it was toward Polynesia that he turned. And in Samoa and Tahiti for a time he did indeed find examples of cultures that represented almost unspoiled civilizations. The vitality and decency of the people Henry Adams got to know well, particularly in Tahiti where—like the infamous John Smith—he was also adopted into the ruling clan, forced him once again to expand his definition of civilization.

---

[47]Ibid.; HA *Diary:* 112, 137, 160.
[48]Ibid., 133, 138, 139.
[49]Ibid., 151.

Anticipating the physical anthropologists who at a much later period dominated the study of different cultures, Adams took extensive bodily measurements of the people he got to know in Polynesia even as he recorded their charms. Yet he did not, like his friend Clarence King, acquire a taste for "old gold" women; in letters he often insisted that he was too old. He certainly enjoyed the young women's uninhibited dancing though, and he frequently regretted the influx of missionaries who had insisted on replacing various stages of native undress with baggy cotton gowns and on substituting drab hymns for classical native dances. Sometimes invoking a literary ancestor, Herman Melville, Adams noted with sorrow the loss of innocence and the physical destruction Westerners had brought to Polynesian cultures. And he attempted to reconstruct the quality of the disappearing world he had known in Tahiti from the point of view of the natives who still lived there.

In the early 1890s, Adams urged his friend Queen Marau to publish her mother Arii Taimai's memoirs as a genealogical record as well as a testimony to a life style that had been lost. The 1901 revised edition, privately printed under Adams's supervision, included a fifteen-page adaptation of the old chiefess's oral history signed by Tauraatua I Amo (Bird Perch of God), the special name bestowed upon Henry Adams by his new family. He was particularly proud to have got one of the best names in the Teva clan; La Farge jested that he had become "more Teva than the Tevas."[50] If being part of such a clan awakened feelings that Adams's European connections never quite permitted, it is significant also that the clan itself demonstrated the power and dignity of the women rulers who had fascinated Henry since the early years of his marriage. The human leadership qualities Adams was always looking for he found in this aristocracy of women and in his new half-Jewish "brother" Tati Salmon, who had taken over the eight Teva districts. "Hebrew and Polynesian mix rather well when the Hebrew does not get the better,"[51] Adams wrote with that part of his mind that was ever hostile to patriarchal society and suspicious of Western civilization. Tati, he complained elsewhere, behaved too much like the Duke of Argyle; yet Adams's letters are full of love and admiration for this unlikely new family. "Life was a double thing," he would insist when he finally tried to understand his own education.[52]

---

[50]Quoted in Ernest Samuels, *Henry Adams: The Major Phase* (Cambridge, Mass., 1964), 44.
[51]Ibid., 42.
[52]*EHA*, 9.

The Memoirs of Arii Taimai E Marama of Eimeo Teriirere of Tooraai Teriinui of Tahiti, as they finally appeared, documented the rise and fall of the Teva clan, a parable perhaps for the fall of the Western civilization Henry Adams knew best, but nevertheless an accurate description of an intricate real world destroyed by that same Western civilization with its diseases, its intrusive capitalism and its self-righteous Christianity. By the 1830s, only five thousand of the original twenty thousand inhabitants remained. Living testimony to Adams's respect for matriarchy, the Tahitian queen was grateful for her Western son's historical expertise. "When England and France began to show us the advantage of their civilization, we were as races went, a great people," she told him; "Hawaii, Tahiti, The Marquesas, Tonga, Samoa, and New Zealand made a respectable figure on the earth's surface, and contained a population of no small size, better fitted than any other possible community for the conditions in which they lived." What Adams helped document was "the social and moral degradation" that came with the advantages of Western civilization. Not with Western eyes, but with the vision of Queen Marau, he described the limited cultural understanding of such past invaders as Captain Cook. Expanding the anthropological consciousness of the fewer than fifty readers who would possess the text in his lifetime Adams recorded the words of his Tahitian mother: "Until one has dismissed from one's mind the notion of Government such as Europeans conceived it, one must always misunderstand the South Seas."[53]

That Henry Adams transcended so much of his New England Anglo-Saxon upbringing to speak to that multicultural tradition we now call anthropological stems, I feel certain, from his deep commitment to democracy. Looking for "force" or power in human society, he turned away from the political corruption he witnessed daily and from the great numbers of new immigrants he thought indifferent to the traditions of the best and brightest, which he wanted to preserve. Curiously, his anthropological vision grew out of his "habit of doubt" about his own culture. His scholarship—from his early work on Pocahontas to his final survey of Tahiti—served to reinforce his political skepticism even as it clarified his human values. He had learned not only to distrust his own judgment but to reject "totally" the judgment of the world.[54]

---

[53]Quoted in *HA: The Major Phase*, 107; *Tahiti*, ed. Robert E. Spiller (collation of 1895 & 1901 eds., New York, 1947), 6.
[54]*EHA*, 6.

Finding himself an outsider in the society his family had helped to create, Adams chose—as many of our greatest writers have done—to identify with the powerless and exotic: the Woman, the Native American, the Buddhist, and finally the Tahitian Queen. A "double consciousness" burdened him as surely as it did W. E. B. DuBois, the inventor of the term derived from Emerson. In the end—even as he yearned for the cultural unity he saw in other worlds, Henry Adams's committed openmindedness forced him to confront the value of multiplicity as part of his own identity as an American.

HENRY ADAMS AND THE AMERICAN ARTISTS: THE TWO MANSIONS

Paul R. Baker

Amidst the poses, self-questionings, ironies, and speculations of Henry Adams's *Education*, the reader is struck here and there by certain relatively straightforward appraisals that provide benchmarks within this autobiography of sorts. One such appraisal forming a point of reference in *The Education* is that of the American figures, most of them artists, men of his own generation, and of the one following, who, Adams suggested, had made names for themselves in the world: Richard Morris Hunt, William Morris Hunt, Henry Hobson Richardson, John La Farge, Augustus Saint-Gaudens, Charles Follen McKim, and Stanford White are named, along with the writers Bret Harte and Henry James and the clergyman Phillips Brooks. These, Adams wrote, were men "who counted as a force even in the mental inertia of sixty or eighty million people."[1]

Adams's visit to the Chicago World's Fair in 1893 occasioned in *The Education* another assessment of American artists. At the Exposition, Adams was struck by the unified neo-classical dress of the great White City and wondered whether "this sharp and conscious twist toward ideals" in architecture was "real or only apparent." If this new artistry were real and "if the people of the Northwest actually knew what was good when they saw it, they would some day talk about Hunt [chairman of the Board of Architects and designer of the administration building] and Richardson, La Farge and St.-Gaudens [a consultant], Burnham [the chief architect of the fair] and McKim, and Stanford White [both of whom designed buildings] when their politicians and millionaires were otherwise forgotten." Then, later on, discussing the Paris Exposition of 1900, Adams once more brought up most of

---

[1]Henry Adams, *The Education of Henry Adams* (New York, 1931), 315. For a discussion of Adams's relations with American artists, see Ernst Scheyer, *The Circle of Henry Adams: Art & Artists* (Detroit, 1970). See also Marc Friedlaender, "Henry Hobson Richardson, Henry Adams, and John Hay," *Journal of the Society of Architectural Historians*, 29 (1970): 231-246.

the same names—Saint-Gaudens, Richardson, La Farge, the Hunt brothers, and White. These were American figures, whom Adams, it would seem, greatly respected.[2]

Henry Hobson Richardson was the first of these American artists whom Adams came to know. During his "wasted years" at Harvard College, Adams later recalled he "made no acquaintance there that he valued in after life so much as Richardson." Adams's Southern-born classmate's mother was a granddaughter of the famous English theologian and scientist Joseph Priestley, and Richardson had spent a comfortable childhood on the family plantation in Louisiana and in New Orleans. After leaving Harvard, a year after Adams, Richardson went on to France, where, in Paris, he was admitted to the Ecole des Beaux-Arts on his second try at the entrance examinations in 1860, one of the first Americans to study there. He returned to the United States briefly in 1861-1862, and on going back to Paris worked intermittently at the Ecole. During these years, Henry Adams, while serving as secretary to his father in London, occasionally sought out Richardson in Paris and on his visits was introduced to the bohemian world of the Beaux-Arts students. Richardson returned to the United States to establish an architectural practice in New York City in 1866, joining in partnership with Charles Gambrill in 1867. His earliest professional designs in French Second Empire and English Victorian Gothic styles were similar to what other American architects were creating in the late 1860s and early 1870s.[3]

The turning point of Richardson's career came in 1872 with the award to him of the commission for Trinity Church, erected on Copley Square in Boston. In this project the young architect utilized his already developing personal Romanesque style in a striking composition, which brought him widespread recognition and largely set the course for the remainder of his relatively short career. Charles Follen McKim, a young architect recently returned from the Ecole des Beaux-Arts, was employed by Richardson in New York from 1870 to 1872 as chief draftsman of the small firm and in this capacity was largely responsible for the competition drawings for Trinity Church. Young Stanford White, also in Richardson's office, prepared the working drawings for the project. As the Trinity commission went forward, Richardson in 1874 moved his studio-office and home from New

[2]Adams, *Education*, 340-341, 385-386.
[3]Ibid., 54, 64, 213.

York to Massachusetts, renting a house in Brookline from Henry Adams's brother-in-law, Edward Hooper. Adams occasionally saw Richardson socially in the Boston area while, until 1877, he was on the Harvard faculty. As the church neared completion, Richardson engaged John La Farge to work on the interior decoration, and Augustus Saint-Gaudens was briefly employed there as a painter. Adams followed the course of design and construction of Trinity Church with great interest, its decoration later reflected in the pages of his novel *Esther*.

Richardson was a man of tremendous vitality, boundless energy, and infectious enthusiasm, who made a strong impression on his clients, his fellow architects, and his friends. His wit and humor, warm smile, and slight stammer charmed those about him. To Adams, Richardson had such an "overflow of life" that he was, indeed, "irresistible."[4]

From 1866 to 1886, Richardson completed some 150 designs, of which about 86 were built, including structures for most major American needs of the time—churches, libraries, stores, banks, commuter railroad stations, government buildings, memorials and monuments, education buildings, and private houses. Among the best-known of his works are the New York State Capitol at Albany, the Allegheny County Courthouse in Pittsburgh, the Marshall Field Wholesale Store in Chicago, and Sever and Austin Halls at Harvard (the latter two, both negotiated by the Harvard treasurer Edward Hooper). In 1885, a poll of professional architects choosing the ten best American buildings, put Trinity Church in first place of the ranking, with four other Richardson buildings among the top ten. A century later, in 1982, an architects' poll of the best American buildings again put Trinity among the top five choices.[5]

It was Richardson's work on private houses that Henry Adams came to know best in the 1880s. While Henry and Marian Adams were living "the golden years" in Washington, D. C., as Henry worked on his *History*, Richardson frequently came to the national capital to consult with Nicholas Anderson, a classmate from Harvard College, for whom he was building a large house on K Street at Sixteenth Street. Henry and Marian saw a good deal of Richardson on his visits to Washington. The Adamses closely and with

---

[4]Harold Dean Cater, *Henry Adams and His Friends* (New York, 1970), 240; J. C. Levenson et al., eds., *The Letters of Henry Adams* (Cambridge, Mass., 1982), 3: 486.

[5]Jeffrey Karl Ochsner, *H. H. Richardson: Complete Architectural Works* (Cambridge, Mass., 1982), 9; James F. O'Gorman, *H. H. Richardson: Architectural Forms for an American Society* (Chicago and London, 1987), 29-53 and passim; "The Ten Best Buildings," *American Architect and Building News*, 17 (13 June 1885): 282-283; *Preservation News* (May 1982), 2.

fascination followed the course of construction of the $100,000 Anderson house in 1882-1883. The firm lines, the low-arched entryways, the round projecting corner bay, the deeply-set windows, and the variegated brickwork gave the house a massiveness and dignified simplicity that set it apart from the fussy Victorian design of most contemporary dwellings. The Adamses were tremendously impressed with the Anderson mansion: Marian considered it "emphatically a gentleman's house . . . very stern and severe as a whole," but Henry praised it as "a gem . . . the handsomest and most ultimate house in America" and "the only one [he] would like to own." Marian took photographs of the Anderson house, and she and her husband were the first guests there after it was completed. Close by on K Street, Richardson began in 1885 a house for Benjamin Warder, in a similar style; it was very large and in some ways even more impressive.[6]

Soon after the Anderson house was completed, Adams's one-time Harvard colleague and brother-in-law Professor Ephraim Gurney and his wife Ellen, who was Marian's sister, in October 1884 commissioned Richardson to design for them a country house in Beverly Farms, on Boston's north shore. A rectangular structure, with a large service wing adjoining the central mass, covered by steeply pitched roofs, and with two porches, the Gurney house was most characterized by the rugged glacial boulders of the exterior walls. The Gurney house, Adams once remarked, looked "like the cave of Polyphemus or any other fellow." A year before the Gurney house was begun, in 1883, Dr. Robert William Hooper, Marian's father, also commissioned Richardson to design a small addition to his summer house in Beverly, Massachusetts. The addition was to include a study and a playroom, but there is no evidence that design was executed.[7]

With the Adamses' long-standing friendship with Richardson and their close acquaintance with the Anderson house, their choice of Richardson as architect for their own new residence in Washington was almost inevitable. When a site facing Lafayette Square on H Street at the corner of Sixteenth became available, Adams suggested to his close friend John Hay that the location would be ideal for two adjoining houses. Hay purchased the plot and in turn sold a part of it to Adams. Planning on the Hay and Adams houses began in January 1884, and by July the foundations

---

[6]Ochsner, *Richardson*, 256-260, 374-378; Ward Thoron, ed., *The Letters of Mrs. Henry Adams, 1865-1883* (Boston, 1937), 295, 395; Levenson et al., eds., *Letters*, 2: 508, 525; Friedlaender, 236.

[7]Ochsner, *Richardson*, 368-371, 308; Levenson et al., eds., *Letters*, 2: 627.

were being laid. Both owners submitted suggestions for their res-
idences to Richardson, and Henry and Marian became deeply
involved in the planning process. Many letters passed between
clients and architect. As construction and decoration went on,
Richardson occasionally came to Washington to inspect the
double-house project.[8]

Like most Richardsonian buildings, the two houses were thick-
walled, with the window and door openings deeply recessed.
Above a light-colored, roughly finished Ohio sandstone base, the
walls were covered by bricks in various shapes and sizes and laid
in several patterns. The two separate but attached houses were
clearly differentiated, with their entrances on different streets.
On the much larger Hay house, facing on Sixteenth Street, the
rounded corner of the house was echoed by the hexagonal stair
tower to the right of the gabled entrance bay. The principal decorative interest, on the side facade, lay in a deeply recessed loggia, faced with heavy columns, and, above, a large opening
forming another loggia, and, on the front, the Syrian arch entry-
way, echoing entryways for the Trinity Church rectory and Sever
Hall. Inside the Hay house, the large central hallway, with its
elegant, cascading, paneled staircase, provided a central core
from which the reception rooms and spaces for public entertainment opened.[9]

The Adams house, facing south at 1603 H Street, was smaller
and more delicately conceived, though it was a substantial townhouse and embodied the rugged strength of the Hay house.
Henry and Marian liked to downplay the size and character of
their new house, as it was being built, referring to it, on occasion,
as a "Spartan little box." The four-story Adams house rested on
asymmetrically placed cave-like archways at the ground level, the
main entry to the right and a service door on the left, the arches
laced with carvings and resting on clustered colonnettes. On the
upper floors, the many windows facing south let in an abun-
dance of light. A cave-like loggia at the third-floor level echoed a
similar element on the Hay house and repeated the theme established below at the street level. Within the Adamses' dwelling,
the library, study, and dining room were placed on the principal
floor in an L around the staircase at the side. Hay and Adams
were quite aware of the cave-like appearance of some of the open-

---

[8]Ochsner, *Richardson*, 344-349; Scheyer, *Circle of Henry Adams*, 164-170; Friedlaender, 241-
242; for one such letter, see Levenson et al., eds., *Letters*, 2: 546.

[9]Henry-Russell Hitchcock, *The Architecture of H. H. Richardson and His Times*, rev. ed.
(Cambridge, Mass., 1977), 270-271.

ings of their new houses, and at times referred to themselves as "troglodytes," or cave-dwellers.[10]

Tragically, on 6 December 1885, shortly before the Adams residence was ready for occupancy, Marian Adams took her own life. Despite his loss, Henry determined to retain the house, which he and his wife had planned together, and he moved in by 17 December, resolved to go "straight ahead without looking behind." Interior finishing, decoration, and furnishing went on for some time, and no doubt the day-to-day work helped Henry through the terrible weeks that followed. The house was comfortable and suited his needs, and it remained his principal home for the remainder of his life. In his new dwelling, Henry Adams had a centrally located cave into which he could crawl, hidden away from the world outside.[11]

Within a few weeks, "the big and jolly" Richardson also was dead. The architect had long suffered from severe, chronic kidney disease and the discomfort of hernias; he had become vastly corpulent, ultimately weighing some 345 pounds. Despite his illness, he overindulged in food and drink, a customary way of life for years; when counseled that moderation was necessary, he was unwilling and possibly unable to make a change. As his health deteriorated in his final months he kept largely to his room, getting out of bed only around noon. On infrequent visits to works under construction, he had to be taken everywhere by carriage, even for only a few steps. He died on 27 April 1886, at the age of forty-seven.

Adams's working relationship with Richardson had provided him a sometimes frustrating introduction to the practices of architects. Everything had moved more slowly than Adams had anticipated, and very likely the cost had considerably exceeded preliminary estimates, for Richardson regularly insisted on "extravagances," not all of which, Adams came to realize, could be eliminated.

Frustrations with delay and with the ways of artists were also evident in the creation of what Adams later called "my mansion at Rock Creek." What eventuated from this second commission was, however, far more interesting and significant as a work of art than the dwelling that Richardson had created for him. The Adams Memorial figure in Washington's Rock Creek Cemetery is widely acknowledged as the greatest achievement of the most

---

[10]Friedlaender, 232, 242.
[11]Levenson et al., eds., *Letters*, 2: 643-644.

important late nineteenth-century American sculptor, Augustus Saint-Gaudens. The work is immensely enhanced by its architectural setting, designed by Stanford White.[12]

Adams first became acquainted with Saint-Gaudens and White during the mid-1870s, when Saint-Gaudens briefly assisted with the decoration of Trinity Church and young White worked under Richardson out of the Brookline office. Of the two artists, White was decidedly the more colorful. Stanford White, unfortunately, is better remembered today for the manner of his death than for his important body of architectural and decorative work and his significant impact on the face of New York City. He was murdered on 25 June 1906, by the crazed husband of White's one-time mistress, on the roof garden of Madison Square Garden, which he himself had designed. Titillating tales of White's secret bohemian life and exaggerated estimates of his artistic productivity since his death have become embedded in American popular lore—and boost real estate sales even today.

White came from a family, like that of Henry Adams, with New England roots stretching back to the seventeenth century. His father was a prominent New York journalist, music and literary critic, and Shakespeare scholar, who, like Adams, deplored the materialism, the corruption, and the democratic leveling of post-Civil War America. Richard Grant White, the father, like Adams, was perpetually dissatisfied with his country, with his city, and with himself.

After contemplating but rejecting a career as a painter, young Stan entered Richardson's office in 1870, when he was only sixteen and remained there for eight years. Tall—at six feet three inches, he towered a foot over tiny Henry Adams—with bristling, closely cropped red hair and a large bushy mustache, Stan received splendid architectural training under Richardson. In 1878, White left his position for an extended visit to Europe. He returned to New York in the fall of 1879 to join with Charles McKim and William Rutherford Mead, from Vermont, in a new architectural firm, McKim, Mead & White. From its beginning the partnership flourished, with many commissions, largely from wealthy, socially prominent New Yorkers, often personal friends of the architects. Most of White's best-known projects, such as the Washington Memorial Arch, the Judson Church and Tower, the Herald Building, the Tiffany and Gorham buildings, Madison Square Presbyterian Church, and many large mansions came after his work on the Adams Memorial.

---

[12]Ibid., 2: 537, 553, and 5: 325.

Augustus Saint-Gaudens, five and one-half years older than White, was born in Dublin, Ireland, in 1848, to a French father, who crafted fine shoes, and an Irish mother. He was brought to the United States as a baby and grew up in New York, apprenticed to cameo cutters and educated for a time at the Cooper Institute and at the National Academy of Design. In 1867, he went to Paris to study at the Ecole des Beaux-Arts, followed by work in Rome. Soon after the sculptor's return to New York in 1875, White, while visiting a Fourteenth Street building, heard someone bellowing out operatic arias, went to investigate the source of the noise, and encountered the sharp-featured, red-haired man who soon became his best friend and artistic collaborator.

Two years later, in 1877, Saint-Gaudens was married and almost immediately left New York for Paris to set up a studio and work there on various commissions. On White's visit to Europe, he made the Saint-Gaudenses' apartment his headquarters for excursions into the French countryside. In Paris, the two friends worked together on a monument honoring Admiral David G. Farragut, which was finally completed and unveiled in Madison Square Park in May 1881, following Saint-Gaudens's return to settle in New York.

The Farragut Monument was a resounding success, with a remarkable integration of sculptural and architectural elements. The figure of the admiral still stands today in the park firmly resolute, with feet wide apart, as if on a rolling deck, a realistic portrait figure in an admiral's uniform, the coat flung aside by the wind, set on a pedestal of almost art nouveau design, with low relief figures, incised flowing waves, and a long inscription composed by White's journalist father.

The two artists soon gained other major commissions for monuments and statuary work, mostly realistic with the architecture and sculpture closely integrated. In Chicago, a committee arranging for a statue honoring Abraham Lincoln, was so inspired by the Farragut that the members determined to have Saint-Gaudens undertake their project. The *Standing Lincoln*, on which White collaborated, was completed in October 1887. Set on a granite pedestal on a broad platform, the dignified figure of the president stands before a chair, his head slightly bowed, lost in thought. A sixty-foot bench curves behind and enframes the statue.

Simultaneously, the two artists were engaged in a commission for Springfield, Massachusetts, a figure of Deacon Samuel Chapin, a seventeenth-century founder of the city. Known as *The Puritan*, the statue was unveiled in November 1887. Set on a circular base, the heroic bronze figure of Deacon Chapin, his cloak blown back, strides forward as if going to church, a Bible grasped in his left arm and a walking staff in his right hand.

The best-known collaboration of the two artist-friends came in New York at about the same time as the Adams Memorial project, for one of the most prominent sites in the city. Diagonally to the northeast of Madison Square, White designed Madison Square Garden, a large entertainment center, in a Spanish Renaissance mode. The large amusement palace included an indoor arena, a theater, a concert hall, an open-air roof garden, and space for restaurants. The most striking architectural feature of the Garden was the tower, rising some 340 feet, with upper viewing platforms and seven stories of small apartments, one of which White himself rented as a hideaway. To cap the tower, White asked Saint-Gaudens to create a statue figure.

Diana, goddess of hunting and of the moon, was an eighteen-foot idealized figure of beaten sheet copper fastened to a wrought-iron pipe frame. The full-breasted goddess was set on a crescent moon of plate glass, lighted from within by incandescent lamps, and she rotated like a weathervane with the wind. When Diana was raised to the uppermost pinnacle of the tower in 1891, she immediately became one of the most famous of New Yorkers. Crowds gathered in the park below gazing up at the "golden girl," though some critics complained that an unclothed figure was not at all proper so prominently displayed. When the statue was in place, White was, however, dismayed by the disproportionate size of the figure to the tower. Eventually, Diana was taken down and sent off to the Chicago Fair to perch atop McKim's Agriculture Building. At their own expense, the two artists had a second, smaller Diana, some thirteen feet tall, crafted and placed atop the tower in late 1893.

Contrasting considerably with these commissions was the Adams Memorial. Henry Adams commissioned the monument to his wife while in New York in June 1886, as he was setting out for the Far East. As was often the case with Saint-Gaudens's work, the project moved slowly; the sculptor did not commence preparing preliminary drawings until late the next year. For some time, even White did not get to see Gus's sketches and plaster models, and when finally he did, he objected to references in some drawings and models to Socrates, who had committed suicide. Adams, in consultation with John La Farge, his guest companion on the trip to Japan, had wanted something of an Oriental character in the work, though he surmised that neither Saint-Gaudens nor White had real understanding of Oriental art. As the sculptor developed his ideas, Michelangelo's Sistine Chapel lunette figures, it turned out, were an important influence on his conception, and in the position of the veil and the right hand, the new work also referred back to a wedding plaque that Saint-Gaudens had made of Bessie White as a wedding present for Stanford and his bride in 1884 (Metropolitan Museum of Art). The veil and face also recall an early statue, *Silence*, which Saint-Gaudens had created in Rome in 1874 (Masonic Soldiers' and Sailors' Hospital, Utica, N. Y.). White kept in close touch with Adams about the progress of the work, and at one time sent the historian a present of a large salmon he had caught at his fishing camp in Canada, a characteristic gift he often made to favored clients. But the project went so slowly that at times Adams wondered if the work would ever be finished. Eventually in the fall of 1890, carving and polishing of the stonework took place, and the figure was finally set up and the work mostly completed in March 1891, while Adams was traveling, once again with La Farge, in the South Pacific.[13]

Before Adams eventually saw the monument in place, he was highly critical of the two artists, writing to his confidante Elizabeth Cameron that nothing had distressed him so much as Saint-Gaudens's and White's "outrageous disregard of [his] feelings in the matter," complaining, in effect, of the long delays. Whimsically, he suggested that he would like to club them over their heads "and put them under their own structure." When, however, his next-door neighbor John Hay reported enthusiastically by letter to him on the monument, Adams expressed relief and wrote back that from the photographs sent him, the memorial was "at least not hostile" to his own conceptions.[14]

Surrounded by a thick, enveloping wall of holly shrubs and cedar trees, the Adams Memorial rests on a hexagonal platform some twenty by twenty-eight feet. The mysterious, brooding, androgynous figure, shrouded under a cloak, the face resting on the right arm and hand, is seated on a boulder, with a stone footrest. A polished pink granite stele topped by moldings forms a backdrop to the figure. Opposite the statue, around the edges of the platform, is a stone bench, where visitors can sit, shut away from the world outside and contemplate the figure. The memorial has no inscriptions.

Adams's later feelings about the memorial became more positive. He often went there and sat on the bench, watching visitors

---

[13]Ibid., 3: 494, 160, 126, 415, 416.
[14]Ibid., 3: 406, 494.

and listening to their comments: the figure itself, he discovered, stimulated self-revelatory responses from the viewers. Both Adams and Saint-Gaudens considered that the name "The Peace of God" was appropriate for the work, though in time Adams believed that any name was too limiting. In a letter to Saint-Gaudens's son, Homer, Adams asked that the younger Saint-Gaudens not "allow the world to try [the] figure with a name! Every magazine writer wants to label it as some American patent medicine for popular consumption—*Grief, Despair, Pear's Soap,* or *Macy's Men's Suits Made to Measure.*" The sculptor, Adams insisted, had meant the figure to pose a question, not to provide an answer.[15]

Adams, it is evident, came to appreciate and even enjoy his two homes in Washington, both the H Street townhouse and the "mansion in Rock Creek." Both of these "mansions" fitted his needs well. Adams wanted to be near the center of things: he liked to be close to his ancestors' home, across Lafayette Park, where important national decisions were made. He enjoyed having a few select friends about him, whom he could see in his own comfortable quarters. At the same time, though, he had on occasion a strong need to isolate himself, to shut himself off from the outside world. The structure that Richardson built for him facing Washington's central square provided both a place to receive friends and a place of retreat. There, as a cave-dweller, he could, indeed, crawl into his cave, bar the entrance, and withdraw from the world. The other "mansion," where Marian lay, though not inaccessible to strangers, was also secluded from the outside world. (The memorial is still hard to find for anyone not informed of its precise location.) With a tunnel-like, corridor entrance through the thick screening of shrubbery and trees, the memorial provided Adams with another place of refuge, where he could hide. Richardson, Saint-Gaudens, and White in crafting the two mansions had served Adams well.

These three along with the other American artists mentioned in *The Education,* it is apparent, were men whom Adams admired. The architects Richardson, White, Richard Morris Hunt, and Daniel Burnham were strikingly similar in personality—all of them dominating figures, men bursting with vitality, energy, and enthusiasm. Hunt and White were renowned for their picturesque, expletive-filled speech. And throughout his adult life, White emulated his teacher-employer Richardson in over-

---

[15]Adams, *Education,* 329; Cater, *Henry Adams,* 609-610.

indulgence in food and drink, carefree spending of money, lavish collecting of art objects, and sensual aestheticism. Moderation was alien to both of them. All four were big men, heavy-set. All towered over dainty, little Henry Adams. All were knowledgeable about business affairs and highly successful professionally. Charles McKim, in contrast to these others, was quiet, fastidious, often prim, sometimes self-effacing, but always charming to those about him, rather like Adams himself. Saint-Gaudens was rather different in some ways from the others, too, and struck Adams as remarkably inarticulate, lacking in knowledge of the world, indeed something, as Adams put it, of "a simple minded babe," though, just the same, a remarkable artist-teacher. No doubt the sculptor at times was ill at ease with the intellectual Adams, for his own formal education had been very limited. With his closest friends, Saint-Gaudens liked to "whoop it up," and for years he was a regular companion of Stanford White in nights on the town, very much the physical sensualist as well as the aesthete.[16]

To the carefully spoken, introspective, acutely sensitive Henry Adams, there was in these American artists, who were spilling over with vitality, mostly loud, often raunchy and vulgar, unreflective (except for La Farge and William Morris Hunt), much that Adams greatly esteemed. They were men deeply involved with their own times, living fully in the world, in ways that Adams temperamentally could not. But unlike many others caught up in the world—businessmen, politicians and statesmen, even, perhaps, novelists and historians, whose books might be laid away on library bookshelves—these American artists were creating tangible things—buildings, statuary, and paintings—that would last beyond them and be noticed. Like the anonymous builders of the great French cathedrals, these American artists were creating physical objects that future generations would have to come to terms with. In their works, in their creative acts, these American artists accounted themselves to themselves, and, in effect, invented formulas of their own for the universe. And *that* was something Adams felt deeply about.[17]

---

[16]Cater, *Henry Adams*, 423.
[17]Adams, *Education*, 472.

A DISSENTING VIEW OF JOHN QUINCY ADAMS

Peter Shaw

John Quincy Adams, the oldest son in the second of four famous Adams generations, cast his shadow over the family in both directions. From the beginning his parents, John and Abigail Adams, were impressed by his obedience and prodigious capacity for study. Eventually they were all but overwhelmed by pride in his career, which became the focus of their lives. John Quincy subsequently quite overshadowed his own sons, the third Adams generation, until they were well into middle age.

The most prominent of them, Charles Francis Adams, had a short political career of his own, and then devoted twenty years to editing his father's immense diary. Though Charles Francis lived a typically long Adams life, he did not have enough time left over to undertake the task that he had set himself of writing John Quincy's biography. His son Brooks did have the time and did complete a biography—with results discussed further on in this essay.

John Quincy's career stretched for over fifty years from the early 1790s to 1848 when he collapsed on the floor of the United States Congress a few hours before his death. Adams served as a diplomat, senator, secretary of state, president, and congressman. He produced a vast record of his period in the diary that he kept nearly every day of his life from adolescence onward. This was the work that took his son Charles Francis Senior twenty years to edit. John Quincy also left an array of valuable letters, both public and private, as well as public documents written and recopied in his own hand. He wrote translations, lectured on rhetoric at Harvard, composed perhaps twenty volumes of poetry from which he selected two slim volumes for publication, and distinguished himself in science with his masterly "Report on Weights and Measures."

As a historian, Henry Adams frequently employed his grandfather's papers. He edited and introduced some of them to the public, and quoted extensively from still others in his biographies and his multi-volume *History* of the United States from 1800 to 1817. Yet Henry Adams's scholarly career can be described as a tiptoeing around direct confrontation with his grandfather. Always in Henry's books, John Quincy Adams appeared in the course of someone else's life or someone else's presidential administration. He was treated in a favorable but subsidiary way, as when to illustrate the career of Albert Gallatin, he is included with that politician as one of the "last relics of the early statesmanship of the republic."[1]

Henry revealed a different view in 1909, after receiving from his brother Brooks a manuscript biography of their grandfather, along with a request for a critical reading. Henry replied with a detailed, monograph-length, chapter by chapter commentary and a letter. Neither his commentary nor Brooks's manuscript biography have ever been published.

Brooks had labored "to save the family reputation for the next generation," as he put it, but Henry disapproved of the resultant biography, which was both unfinished and unfocused.[2] Henry's method of discouraging Brooks was elaborately to praise him, characterizing his own views as mere student-like epitomes of the biography's argument. By this means Henry twisted Brooks's implied praise of John Quincy so as to reflect his own unfavorable judgment. Brooks somewhat weakly replied that he had not really intended to be interpreted in this way. He protested that he personally held a much higher estimate of John Quincy than Henry seemed to suppose. But Brooks conceded his failure to convey this opinion convincingly when he stated that "a biographer should try to put himself in the skin of his subject and show the man as the man saw the world about him. My own opinions are of no importance."[3]

Henry had in fact called on Brooks not for opinions but for scientific history and aesthetic form, both of which he had succeeded in incorporating in his own biographical and historical writing. He asserted now that for all John Quincy's historical importance, he had been a man standing on the outskirts of events, "following the march of forces which he never commanded."[4]

---

[1]Henry Adams, *The life of Albert Gallatin* (New York, 1943), 496–497.

[2]Paul C. Nagel, *Descent From Glory: Four Generations of the Adams Family* (New York and Oxford, 1983), 351: the only account that gives full weight to the severity of Henry Adams's critique.

[3]Brooks Adams to Henry Adams, 6 March 1909, Houghton Library, Harvard University.

[4]Henry Adams to Brooks Adams, 18 Feb. 1909, *The Letters of Henry Adams*, ed. J. C. Levinson et al. (Cambridge, Mass., 1988), 6: 226. This letter is followed by Henry's comments keyed to the page numbers of the Ms. biography; these numbers appear in the

Brooks himself had previously borrowed from Henry the notion of historical forces, vastly refining and elaborating it into an interpretive method. If he intended to present this biography to the world, Henry was suggesting, he would be obliged to look at John Quincy in the light of some such method.

Henry also suggested that a biography of John Quincy without opinions was bound to result in boredom. The man could be rescued only by art and a bit of guile on the part of his biographer. Despite his praise of Brooks, then, Henry was saying that the biography was inadequate as written. Brooks was left with the option of revising, but was faced at every turn with Henry's disturbing but persuasive negative view. The result was that Brooks set the manuscript aside until after Henry's death. Then, in a memorial volume for Henry, he quoted from Henry's letter, and declared his "dissent" from its withering criticisms of John Quincy.[5] Instead of answering these, though, he offered a new version of their grandfather's career. John Quincy Adams now became not so much a statesman as America's foremost man of science since Franklin. John Quincy's signal achievements became the writing of his "Report on Weights and Measures" while secretary of state and his long-range vision of public works and a program of scientific advancement for America while president.

Henry's critique addressed itself to a few turning points and signal events in John Quincy's career. His early years as a diplomat in Europe from 1794 to 1801 were relatively unimportant. But during the term in the Senate to which Adams was appointed in 1803, he supported the embargo imposed in 1807 by Jefferson (the man who had defeated John Adams for the presidency), in retaliation for British impressments of American seamen. Adams's support of this measure led to his expulsion from his father's Federalist party, followed by his joining Jefferson's Republican party.

Soon after this, Adams was returned to diplomacy by his new party, serving long years in Russia and—like his father before him—in England. He also led the American delegation that signed the peace treaty with England bringing to an end the War of 1812. In 1817 Adams returned to the United States to serve as secretary of state under James Monroe. He exerted a crucial influence on American foreign policy by drawing up the terms of the Monroe Doctrine and by negotiating with Spain for the ces-

---

upper left hand corners of Henry's pages. Since the comments on each page run to several pages themselves, in the notes that follow the page referring to Brooks's biography is given first, followed by the page number of Henry's sequence of comments on it. Houghton Library.

[5]Brooks Adams, "The Heritage of Henry Adams," in Henry Adams, *The Degradation of the Democratic Dogma* (New York, 1919).

sion to the United States of lands ranging from Florida to the Pacific. Adams called the Florida Treaty that accomplished this enormous expansion of American territory "the most important incident of my life and the most successful."[6]

In 1824 Adams was elected to the presidency. He proposed visionary plans for the development of public lands by the government, but was defeated by Andrew Jackson before achieving any success. Adams then surprised his family and official Washington by returning to politics in 1830 in the decidedly less prestigious role of a Massachusetts representative to the lower house of Congress. It was from this platform that he led the eighteen-year-long fight for which he is probably best known and which earned him the title of "old man eloquent." He set himself against the Southern apologists for slavery and those in the North who compromised with them, exhibiting all the high moral conviction and daily doggedness that he had learned from his father and developed in his own career. Impotent at first, in the end he prevailed both procedurally and morally. He did not eliminate slavery or prevent the Civil War, but he emerged as the North's voice of conscience.

Henry began his critique of this career with a kind of mock confession. He had, he wrote, often thought of writing his own biography of John Quincy Adams but had refrained out of anticipation that his readers would say: "Aha! now we see it all! and it is just what we all said at the time! The old man made nothing but a series of blunders so awful that he had to run away and hide. H. A. admits it; he has no case."[7] Exactly what Henry meant by this surprising statement emerged only gradually from his detailed comments.

In the first place, Henry could not "forgive him his vote for the [1807] Embargo." In Henry's estimation John Quincy's senatorial vote for this measure was "hideous." He had voted for the embargo "under the pretence that it was a measure of resistance, although he knew Jefferson better than anyone else did, and (like Hamilton) knew that Jefferson was a temporisor by nature."[8] But support of the embargo was not simply a miscalculation. By the phrase "it is just what we all said at the time," the imagined reader of Henry's imagined biography intended a reference to the political enemies of John Quincy Adams. They had branded his eventual move to the Jeffersonian party as political opportunism, and Henry could not deny the charge. The embargo vote, he told

---

[6]*Memoirs of John Quincy Adams*, ed. Charles Francis Adams (Philadelphia, 1874), 1: 24.
[7]Henry to Brooks, 18 Feb. 1909, 289-8 of commentary.
[8]Ibid., 289-2.

Brooks, was "not so bad" as what followed—"his going to the [Jeffersonian] caucus to nominate a candidate for the opposition party: an act which scandalised even his adoring mother to hot and just remonstrance." In admitting this, Henry hastened to say, he was simply taking Brooks's own point once again—and suffering over it as a family member. "I shall be the only reader," he wrote "who squirms out of his skin at seeing the worst charges of our family members so rigorously proved."[9]

Virtually no accusation could be more devastating to an Adams—or his descendants—than that of political opportunism. John Quincy Adams had always stood forth as the perfect embodiment of the family's commitment to unwavering dedication and principle. Now one of his own descendants was denying him his reputation. In fact, Henry proceeded to deny John Quincy one after another of his distinctions, sometimes confirming the accusations of his enemies, sometimes adding accusations of his own. Thus Henry added to the charge that support for the embargo was rewarded with an appointment as American ambassador to Russia, the personal charge that John Quincy's acceptance of the post amounted to "deserting his self-evident duty in Massachusetts at a time of the utmost difficulty."

Once in Russia, again according to Henry alone, John Quincy failed to join Henry Clay and other politicians at home in patriotic support of the War of 1812. Next he let himself "dawdle on in Russia under one pretence or another, when his mother and father pray him to come home, and he has ceased to be useful where he is." When John Quincy finally returned to America as secretary of state and supported Andrew Jackson's legally questionable invasion of Florida, "his critics could not be blamed for charging it on political ambition." Out of the same motive John Quincy "blinked" the Missouri Compromise according to his severest critic—Henry Adams.[10]

All of this could be made comprehensible only in the aesthetic or literary dimension missing from Brooks's treatment. For in Henry's view, John Quincy's motives were far darker than anyone imagined. In fact, at the beginning of his letter to Brooks, Henry evoked a tragic, Aeschylean vision. He called himself "a blind beetle employed by you to sprawl over the history of the grand-parents, whom I pity with the keenest sympathy, and wish had never been born." Henry soon made clear that in his eyes

---

[9]Ibid., 289-2, 3; 289-5.
[10]Ibid., 289-3; 429-2.

John Quincy's life had resembled a tragedy with "a Shakespear-
ean or Sophoclean plot." When Henry described this tragedy,
though, he gave it a lurid, melodramatic glow: "J. Q. Adams is, to
my artistic fancy, a tragic picture, and his Presidency is the most
tragic shadow of it. He is the prophet who ends in secret murder
and open war, violence and fraud and hideous moral depravity."[11]
Once again the references were cryptic. They could not be to Adams's presidency, which was a quiet one. It seems instead that
Henry had in mind the brutalities of Southerners toward their
slaves and the bloody Civil War that had to be fought to bring
slavery to an end.

Slavery, then, was the key to the life of John Quincy Adams. He
was linked to this tragedy and to the Civil War by his two failures
while secretary of state: not opposing Jackson's Florida invasion
and not denouncing the Missouri Compromise and the Southern
politicians who secured it. "J. Q. A.," Henry wrote, "deliberately
acted as a tool of the slave oligarchy (especially about Florida),
and never rebelled until the slave oligarchy contemptuously cut
his throat."[12] By this reading of events, John Quincy Adams did
everything in his power to gain the presidency. Once in office
his previous political compromises fell in on him. Then, his slen-
der political alliances with the politicians of the South broken,
he finally turned on them. His great crusade against slavery in
the latter part of his life, Henry believed, came only when all else
was lost.

That crusade, nevertheless, did him credit. Still regarding John
Quincy's life from the point of view of an artistic biographer writing a kind of novel or satire or tragedy, Henry said of John Quincy's last eighteen years that they "redeemed everything, and
caused the world to forget the crushing failures of the Senate and
the Presidency." Henry characteristically dashed a certain amount
of cold water on this assessment by arguing that the triumph
came at the expense of John Quincy's earlier political principles.
In the first part of his career he compromised with the South, os-
tensibly in order to preserve the Union. But in his final eighteen-
year fight against the South he threw concern for the Union to the
winds. "Had he been true to his professions," Henry wrote, "he
would have gone with Webster and Clay, and would have tried
to save the Union." With characteristic irony Henry accused
the aged John Quincy of therefore having become "a perfectly

[11]Ibid., i, 3.
[12]Ibid., 429-2.

unscrupulous partisan" without regard for the Union, but added, "I need not say how profoundly thankful I am that he was untrue to his professions."[13]

John Quincy Adams's political inconsistency was for Henry accompanied by yet more deplorable shortcomings of character. To Henry's mind the famous diary left the impression chiefly of "a man difficult to live with." He was "abominably selfish." Furthermore John Quincy suffered from "want of judgment," and a lack of "wit or humor." As a writer he was "diffuse" and constitutionally unwilling to correct his lack of form. As a husband and father, "his dragging his wife to Europe in 1809, and separating her from her children was demonic." As a son he was guilty of "neglect of his father for the sake of his damned Weights and Measures."[14] (Here Henry was referring to John Adams's time of need when John Quincy's mother, Abigail Adams, was dying, as well as to the strains of John Quincy's seven-year separation from his two sons, one of whom later committed suicide.)

Most devastating of all was Henry's attack on John Quincy's vaunted patriotism. The truth as demonstrated by his lingering on in Russia when he was needed at home, was that "he loathed and hated America." Including himself as a casualty of John Quincy's refusal to acknowledge this distaste, Henry declared that John Quincy "never thought of going home without nausea, but he and his son, and his grandchildren, had to be trained to profess a passionate patriotism which very strongly resembled cant." Henry treated the series of lectures on rhetoric that John Quincy had been invited to deliver at Harvard in a similar fashion. The lectures had been attended by distinguished members of Boston society as well as students, and had been published in two volumes. But John Quincy was hardly an orator himself, and the ancient models that he set forth had virtually no contemporary applicability. Brooks had not criticized John Quincy on this score, but Henry pretended that Brooks had displayed him as an absurd figure, "whose highest delight is to lecture boys about a rhetoric of which he never could practice either the style or the action or the voice or the art, and then gloating over his own foolish production in print, instead of rolling on the ground with mortification as his grandchildren would do,—this picture grinds the colors into my aesophagus."[15]

At this point Henry's critique has carried far beyond politics to character, morality, and motive—all matters difficult to evaluate.

---

[13]Ibid., 446-6; 495-7, 8.
[14]Ibid.
[15]Ibid., 7; 289-2.

To complicate the picture, most of Henry's accusations are framed as sins of omission: John Quincy's failure toward his family in going to Russia, his failure patriotically to support the War of 1812, his failure to leave Russia when he should have, and his failure to speak out against the Missouri Compromise. Only switching to the Jeffersonian party in 1808 and supporting Jackson's invasion of Florida are treated as sins of commission.

Henry's indictment, then, is not that of a historian, though he was one, but of an interested—and disappointed—party. In contrast, John Quincy Adams's nineteenth-century biographers Josiah Quincy, John T. Morse, and William H. Seward, regarded him as having had, in Seward's words, a "long and spotless career." Twentieth-century historians have been more critical. George Dangerfield, for example, offered a vivid evocation of the cold and intractable personality of which Adams himself was the severest judge. But Dangerfield concluded: "He was above all a moral man. It is one of the clues to his greatness, which, if one follows it carefully, will lead one faithfully through all the thorns and briars and nettles to the very heart of the labyrinth."[16]

Nor has John Quincy Adams lacked twentieth-century defenders of political acts like supporting the Embargo of 1807 and the Missouri Compromise of 1820. Thus Samuel Flagg Bemis had it that Adams "approved the Missouri Compromise as a practical way of putting the slavery question to sleep for a while to let the Union grow in strength and stature." Marie B. Hecht emphasizes that Adams was strongly anti-slavery, but "gave no opinion on the matter himself, wanting to avoid being drawn into the controversy as long as it could be managed." Hecht does not consider whether such a motive might be judged adversely. As for the earlier embargo, Hecht celebrates Adams's actions in a chapter entitled "A Man of Principle." Similarly, the historian James M. Banner summarizes the attacks on Adams by contemporaries who believed that he supported the embargo out of political ambition, but does not find it necessary to offer any refutation of the charge.[17]

And yet the enemies of John Quincy Adams and his grandson, Henry, were not the only ones who found him ambitious. The

---

[16]William H. Seward, *Life and Public Services of John Quincy Adams*. . . . (Auburn, 1849), 88; George Dangerfield, *The Awakening of American Nationalism: 1815-1828* (New York, 1965), 28. See also Norman A. Graebner, "John Quincy Adams: Empiricism and Empire," in Frank J. Merli and Theodore A. Wilson, eds., *Makers of American Diplomacy: From Benjamin Franklin to Henry Kissinger* (New York, 1974), 106-111.

[17]Samuel Flagg Bemis, *John Quincy Adams and the Union* (New York, 1956), 327; Marie B. Hecht, *John Quincy Adams: A Personal History of an Independent Man* (New York and Toronto, 1972), 309; James A. Banner, *To the Hartford Convention: The Federalists and the Origins of Party Politics in Massachusetts 1789-1815* (New York, 1970), 79.

British ambassador, Stratford Canning, thought he detected in Adams "an ambition causing unsteadiness in his political career." Canning also described attempts by Adams to make himself appear to be infused with "national spirit"—something that recalls Henry's charge of patriotic "cant."[18] Hints such as these suggest that Henry's attitudes might more correctly be termed anticipations of modern skepticism, than the aberrations of old age.

Literary scholars, though, have dismissed Henry's critique on both its political and personal sides. It has been called the "splenetic outburst of an embittered old man," and it has been contended that Henry, who was seventy-one when he wrote about John Quincy Adams to Brooks, "read back into the story all his current discontents." To be sure, Henry's turnabout was striking. Brooks was taken by surprise, and for good reason since apparently Henry had never so much as hinted at such disapproval of their grandfather. Thus, like Brooks, Henry disapproved of the embargo as a supine, half-hearted measure by which Jefferson disgraced the nation. From the fierce Adams point of view, which they shared, national self-respect demanded that British impressments of American sailors and other insulting behavior be responded to with nothing less than a declaration of war. Yet in his *History* he had represented John Quincy's "mistake" much more mildly. There he erred only in voting for an embargo without a clause forcing the procrastinating Jefferson to more decisive action at some specified time.[19]

Henry explained his turnabout as simply revealing long-held convictions. He had, he now averred, always felt put upon when defending John Quincy Adams in public. In fact, each time an Adams ancestor had appeared in one of Henry's books (he named four of them) he had loyally "turned myself inside out like an india-rubber ball to make a case for everybody, and especially for J. Q. A., whose case is the weakest of the lot, at least for me to defend, because I am most interested in profiting from the defense."[20] Henry called himself the most interested party because he felt that he had inherited the very characteristics he condemned in his ancestor.

Further explaining himself, but always adhering to the fiction that his own insights were really those of Brooks, Henry now de-

[18]Stanley Lane-Poole, *The Life of the Right Honourable Stratford Canning* . . . . (London, 1886), 1: 308, 309.

[19]William E. Dusinberre, *Henry Adams: The Myth of Failure* (Charlottesville, 1980), 31. Ernest Samuels, *Henry Adams: The Major Phase* (Cambridge, Mass., 1964), 457. Compare William Dusinberre's comments on J. Q. Adams's "mistake," 28.

[20]Henry to Brooks, 18 Feb. 1909, 289-7 of commentary.

clared that he had been persuaded to reject his old view of John Quincy as a self-confident Puritan in favor of Brooks's new theory. This was, supposedly, that John Quincy Adams turned out to be "a sentimentalist so feeble that under a great strain (as in 1809 and 1829) he lay down and invited the world to walk over him; or ran away and abandoned his friends and supporters." (Henry's references were to John Quincy's departure for Russia and to the short period in 1829 when, after losing the presidency to Andrew Jackson, he had retired to the family home in Quincy and cut off virtually all intercourse with the world.) Henry's reason for condemning John Quincy's "sentimental" withdrawals from conflict was now revealed: "I have always felt in myself the sentimental weakness, and have always avoided responsibility in consequence. The likelihood is great that I inherited some share of the old man's nature because I loathe it so heartily."[21] When he made this confession Henry Adams had been living as a semi-recluse for nearly thirty years following the death of his wife by suicide.

But if Henry's identification with his grandfather was emotional, this did not necessarily make it a mere psychological projection, as the literary scholars would have it. No more was Henry's evident aesthetic recoil from John Quincy necessarily a displaced resentment toward an ungrateful America, as one of them has argued. Van Wyck Brooks convincingly accounted for Henry's estrangement as part of a shift in character between pre-Civil War fathers and their sons of "the younger generation of 1870." Comparing such fathers and sons as the Danas, the Hawthornes, the Agassizes, and Charles Francis Adams senior and junior, Van Wyck Brooks contrasted the "emotionally profound, unconscious" elders with their "retiring and reserved . . . introverted" sons.[22] These sons shunned the public limelight in which their fathers had lived, yet were actually more worldly than their fathers. Thus in common with his brother Charles, though with less resentment, Henry Adams felt a gulf between his own modern sophistication and his father's dour, old-fashioned formality.

How much more extreme, then, was the gulf in sensibility between him and his grandfather, a man who struck his own

---

[21]Ibid., 429-3.

[22]Dusinberre, *Henry Adams*, 31. Van Wyck Brooks, *New England: Indian Summer 1865-1915* (New York, 1940), 186. Brooks may have been drawing upon a letter of Henry to Charles Francis Adams, Jr. of 1896 describing their father as "reflective, yet not self-conscious" and declaring of the older generation that "none of the old crowd was very self-conscious." *Letters of Henry Adams (1892-1918)*, ed. Worthington C. Ford (Boston and New York, 1938), 101.

contemporaries as a figure out of his time—not only the last relic of the statesmanship of the early republic, but also of still earlier, self-denying Puritan times. Most of all, John Quincy's rigid formality, his religiosity, and his pompousness weighed on the self-effacing but worldly and ironic sensibility of Henry. Thus the *Education of Henry Adams*, completed a few years before Brooks's biography, tweaked the aged John Quincy by the nose when it treated him as a somewhat absurd old relic in the eyes of Henry at the age of six or seven. The old man undertakes vague, unfocused agricultural experiments by placing seeds and pits under glass only to forget about them and then start others.[23]

Henry's assessment of John Quincy Adams, then, was influenced by personal feelings of various kinds, and these were reflected in his literary rather than purely historical approach to the man. But it should be remembered that Henry was literary in his historical writings as well, and that these were also influenced by personal feelings—without their being disqualified from a professional hearing.[24] It follows that Henry's scheme for the life of John Quincy Adams—a tragic progression from ambition to failure to redemption—deserves the equally serious, professional scrutiny of historians.

---

[23]*The Education of Henry Adams: An Autobiography* (Boston and New York, 1918), 14.

[24]On the family point of view in Henry's *History* see my "Blood is Thicker Than Irony: Henry Adams' *History*," *The New England Quarterly* 40 (1967): 163-187; and "The War of 1812 Could Not Take Place: Henry Adams' *History*," *The Yale Review* 62 (1973): 554-556.

HENRY ADAMS AND THE EUROPEAN TRADITION
OF THE PHILOSOPHY OF HISTORY

John Lukacs

"A weary Titan of Unity."[1] Thus Henry Adams referred to himself and to the work of his mind throughout his life in his *Education*. His commentators and biographers, very much in the American manner, have often attempted to give definitions of such a unity. Contrary to the ideas of some of his commentators—and of Adams himself—I see a division, as well as a split-mindedness, in Adams's life and in his thinking.

The division is that between Adams the historian and Adams the philosopher of history. Such a division is unusual. There is a connection, a well-nigh inevitable spilling over, in the works of those men who wrote histories and then tried to compose their philosophies of history. In Adams's case the distinction between his history-writing and his philosophizing about history amounts to a real difference, to a definite division. I have a very high regard for Henry Adams the historian, but not for his philosophy of history. I am not only referring to the superb qualities of his nine volumes of the *History of the United States during the Administrations of Thomas Jefferson and James Madison*, but also to his fine biographies of Gallatin and Randolph and, perhaps especially, to his reviews and review-essays written in the 1870s, of books by historians such as Freeman, Maine, Green, Stubbs, Fustel de Coulanges, and many others. They are marked by a maturity that is not only rare but virtually non-existent among historians writing in the fourth decade of their lives, whether in America or in Europe; and by a literary judgment and a quality of style probably without equal in the writings of American historians ever since.[2]

---

[1]Henry Adams, *The Education of Henry Adams* (Boston, 1918), 455.

[2]Example: Adams's review of a text of French history written by Kitchin, an unfortunate English historian: Kitchin "again hops away to another branch of the subject, and chirrups about 'the page in my lady's bower,' and the other commonplaces of chivalry. In comparison with such fine writing, the French series of historical textbooks . . . rise to the dignity

Then came a change: Adams turns away from history, to phi-losophy. I am not a Henry Adams scholar; and I cannot establish definitely when this change occurred: in 1879, when he decided to leave Harvard? in 1885, consequent to the tragedy of the sui-cide of his wife? Is it possible that the generally unimaginative and insufficiently appreciative reception of his *History of the United States* contributed to it? In any event, by 1893 his turning away from history-writing was complete. As Brooks Adams wrote about that year: "Henry thought that we would be crushed. And it was then, as Henry pointed out in his *Education*, that his great effort at thoughts began."[3] Yet his disappointment with the qual-ity of his once fellow-academics (of which there is surprisingly little trace in the *Education*) began much earlier. In a pithy sen-tence he once wrote that "the teaching profession is, like the church and the bankers, a vested interest."[4] (One generation later Walter Rathenau said that there are no specialists, there are only vested interests.)

But besides and beyond this very evident and rather clear-cut division in Adams's life between its portion of history-writing and the portion of philosophizing there is that other, more diffi-cult, problem of Adams's split-mindedness. I must insist that by "split-mindedness" I do not mean what, in the twentieth century, is suggested by the term "schizophrenia." Split-mindedness, al-low me to say, is a very American (and often Russian) phenome-non.[5] Contrary to the Freudian scheme, split-mindedness occurs when a mind is split vertically, not horizontally—that is, on the conscious level, and not between the conscious and the so-called subconscious. It consists of the inclination and, even more, of the ability to maintain two different, and essentially contradictory, sets of ideas and beliefs in one's mind. Johan Huizinga pointed out that this had been typical of some of the Middle Ages, and especially of their late period.

An odd thing about Adams is that—rather unusually—he was to some extent aware of this duality, at least in some instances. It is suffused throughout his medievalism. It is discernible within the text of his famous passages about the Virgin and the Dynamo.

---

of historical monuments. Mr. Kitchen could not do better in a new edition than to omit the whole chapter on feudalism and substitute for it a simple translation of that of the *Moyen Age* by M. Duruy."

[3]Brooks Adams, "The Heritage of Henry Adams," in *The Degradation of the Democratic Dogma* (Boston, 1919), 96.

[4]Ernest Samuels, *Henry Adams: The Major Phase* (Cambridge, Mass., 1964), 144.

[5]An example is Tolstoy, no matter how Isaiah Berlin tried to explain this away (in *The Hedgehog and the Fox*, 1954).

He may have been ironic about himself when he wrote that "my idea of paradise is a perfect automobile going thirty miles an hour on a smooth road to a twelfth-century cathedral"[6] (a statement worthy of Dodsworth, or of Babbitt). Alas, one inevitable component of split-mindedness is self-deception. I am afraid that Adams was not ironic when around the same time he wrote to John Hay that in Normandy he found himself "among my respectable Norman ancestors. . . . Caen, Bayeux, St. Lô, Coutances and Mont Saint-Michel are *clearly* [my italics] works that I helped to build. . . ."[7]

One set of dualities that Henry Adams thought he had recognized and understood (and on which he often insisted) was his view of his own background and vision. He thought of himself as standing on one foot in the eighteenth century and on the other in the twentieth. Yet this was, strangely, a narrow-minded view. The Age of Reason, in late eighteenth-century Boston, was very different from the Age of Reason in Europe. Yes: "reason" at that time still had a spacious meaning, as had the German word "Wissenschaft": science as well as knowledge. But the unfortunate and often undiscriminating New England adulation of "Science" was there from the very beginning, more often than not at the expense of true reason, even in the eighteenth century. The humane mentality, the humane reason of a Dr. Johnson was entirely different from Henry Adams's idea of Reason. In the *Education* he wrote that during his youth he and his brothers had tastes far more "modern" than Dr. Johnson. Yet it is Henry Adams's scientism and not Dr. Johnson's humanism that strikes us as antiquated, corroded, hopelessly dated.

Of course much, if not all, of Henry Adams's scientism was his inheritance from Boston and from his Adams ancestors. Brooks, as was his wont, may have exaggerated his attributions of John Quincy Adams's thought,[8] but he hardly exaggerated when he wrote: "Granting that there is a benign and omnipotent Creator of the world, who watches over the fate of men, [John Quincy

---

[6] Samuels, 255.

[7] Ibid., 215.

[8] Example: "Assuming that there was in existence such a universe and such a benevolent God with whom he could covenant, Mr [John Quincy] Adams went on to explain as a scientific fact that a volume of energy lay stored within the United States, which as an administrator he could have developed, had he been able to work at leisure and had he been supported by his Creator." Or: "Like Moses, and a host of other idealists and reformers, John Quincy Adams had dreamed that, by his interpretation of the divine thought, as manifested in nature, he could covenant with God, and thus regenerate mankind. He knew that he had kept his part of the covenant, even too well. In return, when it came to the test, God had abandoned him and had made Jackson triumph."

Adams's] sincere conviction was that such a Being thinks according to certain fixed laws, which we call scientific laws."[9] *That* was the naive—but also narrow-minded and presumptuous—belief in scientism that Henry Adams had ingested and from which he never departed: "the principle that all history must be studied as a science," as he wrote in his *Letter to American Teachers of History* as late as 1910. In the *Education* he wrote: "Since Gibbon, the spectacle was almost a scandal. History has lost even the sense of shame. It was a hundred years behind the experimental sciences. . . . For all serious purposes, it was less instructive than Walter Scott and Alexandre Dumas."[10] Henry Adams failed to recognize not only that history cannot be studied "scientifically," that is, through the application of the methods borrowed or taken from the physical sciences; in a larger sense, he failed to see that "science" is a part of the history of mankind, not the other way around.

The scientism of Henry Adams was his undoing (as it may be the undoing of the United States). It is this scientism that makes his philosophy of history not merely an oddity, not only antiquated, but worthless. His acceptance of the dogmas of Buckle and Darwin was bereft of the elegant and worldly skepticism with which he looked at the confections of many of his contemporary historians. Perhaps his scientism was the natural reaction of a man who, with all of his honest respect of his ancestors, witnessed the fatal shriveling of the metaphysical illusions, of the rigid biblical beliefs and of the shallow spiritualism of New England. His melancholy recognition of Buckle and Darwin is marked by Adams's pessimism, a mood of near-despair. So he wrote in his *Education:* "The historian must not try to know what is truth, if he values his honesty; for, if he cares for his truths, he is certain to falsify his facts."[11] Facts! This is not an elegant paradox; it is a counsel of despair. Earlier, in the first number of the *American Historical Review,* he wrote: "On the average every history contains at least one assertion of fact to every line. A history like that of Macaulay contains much more than one hundred and fifty assertions or assumptions of fact. If the rule holds good, at least thirty thousand of these so-called facts must be more or less inexact."[12] Facts! Henry Adams, this literary artist and master was not able (or was perhaps unwilling) to understand that his-

---

[9]That is: in the universe Scientific Laws came first, and God thereafter.
[10]*Education*, 305.
[11]Ibid., 382.
[12]*The American Historical Review,* October 1895. "Count Edward de Crillon," cited by Samuels, 150-151.

tory is written (and spoken, and thought, and taught) in words; and, moreover, in words that are not made up by a scientific terminology but words of the common and everyday language; that "facts" cannot be separated from the words that express them; that no "fact" exists by itself but that its meaning depends on its association with other "facts"; that the statement of every "fact" depends on its purpose; that the purpose of historical knowledge is not scientific accuracy but human understanding; that man's knowledge of things and man's knowledge of man (which is what history potentially gives us) are not only two different matters, but that the second has a priority over the first, since they involve two different kinds of knowledge, that is, of thinking.

In 1899, almost a decade after he had finished his *History*, Adams wrote that the nine volumes were only "a fragment of history . . . merely an introduction to our history during the Nineteenth Century . . . the real History that one would like to write was to be built on it, and its merits and demerits . . . could be seen only when the structure, of which it was to be the foundation, was raised."[13] In reality, those nine volumes were (and still are) much more than that. What a history of the American nineteenth century he could have given us! Alas, he turned to his philosophy of history instead.[14]

Henry Adams had, as Ernest Samuels wrote, "scoffed at William James's talk of free will; he and Brooks had flatly asserted that the making of the human mind is mechanical."[15] His two communications to the American historical profession are chock-full with such assertions—dogmatically so:

Any science assumes a necessary sequence of cause and effect, a force resulting in motion which cannot be other than what it is. Any science of history must be absolute, like other sciences, and must fix with mathematical certainty the path which human society has got to follow.[16]

---

[13]William Jordy, *Henry Adams, Scientific Historian* (New Haven, 1952), 16.

[14]But there are traces of Adams's scientism in the *History*, too, especially in volume 4. Example: George Washington "conceived the principle that a consolidated community which should have the energy to cohere must be the product of a social system resting on converging highways" (a statement worthy of a spokesman for the Teamsters). Or, also in volume 4, about Fulton's steamship: "Compared with such a step in progress, the medieval barbarisms of Napoleon and Spencer Perceval signified little more . . . than the doings of Achilles and Agamemnon." (An odd coincidence! In September 1939 Alexander Sachs, a New York banker, convinced Franklin Roosevelt to go ahead with Einstein's proposal to build an atom bomb with the argument that Napoleon had lost his bid for world domination because he had rejected Fulton's proposal to build a fleet of steamships with which he could have invaded England. The argument was complete nonsense: yet its eventual result was the atom bomb.)

[15]Samuels, 209.

[16]"The Tendency of History," Adams's communication to the American Historical Association in 1894, cited by Samuels, 127.

Those of us who read Buckle's first volume when it first appeared in 1857, and almost immediately afterwards, in 1859, read *The Origin of Species* and felt the violent impulse which Darwin gave to the study of natural laws, never doubted that historians would follow until they had exhausted every possible hypothesis to create a science of history.[17]

How could [the historian] deny that social energy was a true form of energy. . . . For human history the essential was to convince itself that social energy, though a true energy, was governed by laws of its own.

. . . the only point requiring insistence is that sixty years of progress in science have only intensified the assertion that vital Energy obeys the laws of thermal energy.

. . . if Thought is capable of being classed with Electricity, or Will with chemical affinity, as a mode of motion, it seems necessarily to fall at once under the second law of thermodynamics as one of the energies which most easily degrades itself, and, if not carefully guarded, returns bodily to the cheaper form called Heat.

Man, as a form of energy, is in most need of getting a firm footing on the law of thermodynamics.[18]

Anthony Trollope, having met George Bancroft, asked: "Did he believe what he was saying?"—a properly skeptical question, since Bancroft was not only a trumpeting bloviator; he was also much of a fraud. Did Adams believe what he was saying? Despite his fine aristocratic irony, despite his sophisticated pessimism, despite his paradoxical and humorous exaggerations in his intimate letters I think that—because of his split-mindedness—he did. Ernest Samuels wrote that "his attitude of desperate humor became the most persistent stance of his later life. One laughed for fear of being obliged to weep."[19] There is some truth in this statement; but not enough. Henry Adams's wit was different from a sense of humor that is not only skeptical but humble, since it issues from a self-deprecating understanding of the limits of human wisdom. In 1892, aboard the liner *Teutonic* (*nomen est omen*) he "was dismayed to notice the social decline in First Class. His two hundred fellow passengers seemed somehow all to be Jews. The ship, however, showed the first indubitable sign of mechanical progress."[20] What is remarkable in this kind of reminiscence is not Adams's snobbery or his developing prejudice

---

[17]Ibid., 124.
[18]"A Letter to American Teachers of History," 1910, ibid., 142, 146, 195, 234. (A sort of forerunner of C. P. Snow's fatuous and celebrated thesis about "The Two Cultures." There is only one culture.)
[19]Samuels, viii.
[20]Ibid., 83-84.

against Jews: it is his unshakable prejudice for seeing evidences of "mechanical progress." Twenty years later he misread the symbolic meaning of the catastrophe of the *Titanic*. He wrote to Elizabeth Cameron that it may affect "the confidence in our mechanical success, but the foundering of the Republican Party destroys confidence in our political system."[21]

A knowledge of history, Henry Adams's near-contemporary Agnes Repplier once wrote, is the best fare for one's imagination. It leads to the understanding of people, to standards of judgment, to an ability to contrast and the right to estimate. Consequently, the political views of that modest literary essayist were almost always excellent, by which I mean that they have stood the test of time. The opposite was often true of Henry Adams, in spite of the strength of his mind, of his visionary power, of his historical learning. His contemporary political judgments were often very wrong. In 1893 he wrote to his brother: "I think we reached the end of the Republic here."[22] In 1895: "Once more we are under the whip of the bankers. Even on Cuba . . . we are beaten and hopeless."[23] This was less than three years before 1898. In 1891 he wrote to Lodge: "America has no future in the Pacific. . . . we could Americanize Siberia, and this is the only possible work that I can see still open on a scale equal to American means."[24] "On a scale equal to American means" here is a matter of risible irony, since Adams wrote this at the very time when he was tape-measuring the breasts of Samoan girls. There *is* something wonderful in the innocent—yes, innocent—descriptions of his pleasures in Samoa, when he is American as well as aristocratic, where his fine, thin, Bostonian esthetic sense condemns the crude practices and ideas of low-church Protestant missionaries in Oceania. But there was that other side of his brain, with his tape-measuring that connects Adams's scientism to the silly primitivist ideas of Margaret Mead fifty years later—and perhaps even to the, alas, prototypically modern American stupidities of Drs. Masters and Johnson with their calibrations of genitalia.

And now to an important point: Adams's obsession with the acceleration of history. At times he had a Spenglerian vision of cyclical determinism, with its ever-recurring symptoms of decline. In 1891 he wrote to Brooks that he saw "the age of Andrew Jackson and the cotton planters much as I see the age of Valois or

---

[21]Ibid., 321.
[22]Brooks, *Heritage*, 89.
[23]Ibid., 98.
[24]Samuels, 28.

Honorius—that is, with profound horror."[25] Writing from Sicily in 1899: "The extinction of Greece came with the extinction of the Greek coinage. When the mines are exhausted and population grows society will go to pieces."[26] (What would he have thought of the credit card?) He agreed with Brooks: the fall of Rome came "because of the silver denarius."[27] The Weary Titan of Unity wore down his mind with his wearisome, because senseless, efforts to arrive at a Mathematical Law that would explain everything. Through his split-mindedness, his philosophy of history amounted to an absurdity: to the search for the perfect and eternally valid marriage between (masculine) Mathematics and (feminine) Spirituality. "The ethereal phase," he wrote, will come "in 1921, when thought will reach the limit of its possibilities."[28] Some limit! Some possibilities! Adams should have heeded Tocqueville, who wrote in the 1830s that the extreme agitation of ideas in the age of democracy amounts to mere appearances on the surface of life, that the very opposite of what people fearful of democracy were predicting, would occur: the true movement of minds would slow down, and a long period of intellectual stagnation would prevail. What Adams saw as the acceleration of history—that is, of human thinking—was merely the mechanical acceleration of what we (perhaps wrongly) call "communications."

Sometime after 1875 Henry Adams began to lose touch with the most significant developments of European thought. This happened despite his wide learning, his knowledge of languages, his assiduous reading of English and German and French historians and scientists. The year 1875 is significant: Adams, who read the German philosophers of his time, was unaware of the distinction that Wilhelm Dilthey made in that year about the essential difference between "Naturwissenschaften" and "Geisteswissenschaften," that is, between man's knowledge of nature and man's knowledge of man—a recognition in which Dilthey was not alone (consider but Nietzsche's essay *Über das Studium der Geschichte*, 1874). Through his somber acceptance of Buckle and Darwin, Adams remained ignorant of what I am wont to call the beginnings of post-scientific thinking—not only of Dilthey and Nietzsche but later of Valéry and Bergson, and surely of Jakob Burckhardt, the great historian and historical thinker and the philosophical and cultural historian of Adams's own lifetime (he

---

[25]Brooks, 10.
[26]Samuels, 204-205.
[27]Brooks, 89.
[28]"The Rule of Phase Applied to History," in *Degradation of the Democratic Dogma*, 308.

died in 1897). It was not only Nietzsche who pronounced caustic aphorisms ("Building systems is childishness"). Burckhardt's profound vision denied the meaning of any attempt to erect a systematic philosophy of history. To the contrary: what Burckhardt attempted to write, and teach, was the historical way of seeing things, a historical philosophy, the very obverse of a philosophy of history. "A philosophy of history," Burckhardt wrote, "is a centaur, a contradiction in terms: for history coordinates, and hence is unphilosophical, while philosophy subordinates, and hence is unhistorical." Instead of cobbling together a system that would establish abstract "laws" governing the patterns of history, Burckhardt was interested in the concrete historicity of knowledge, of consciousness, of thought.

Henry Adams's despairing pessimism was not unlike that of other refined Americans of his times, if not of his exact generation. (Owen Wister or John Jay Chapman come to mind.) He died in the same year in which Oswald Spengler completed his *Untergang des Abendlandes* (whose exact English translation is not merely "The Decline" but "The Sinking of the West"). We may regret that he had not read Burckhardt; but we must thank the Almighty that he was (and that we have been) spared of his reading of Spengler.

Henry Adams the historian deserves our respect—more: he deserves our gratitude. In his histories and in his reviews of other historians Henry Adams represented a maturity of learning and a style whereof the flowering of New England was once capable. Henry Adams the philosopher of history has nothing to teach or tell us. This is not only due to Adams's extreme scientism, which is (or obviously should be) antiquated and outdated by now. For the most dangerous and corruptible inclination of the American national mind and character is not really materialism. The speculations of Henry Adams should warn us against a deeper American danger: that of a split-mindedness, which includes the evils of a maddeningly abstract spiritualism running rampant.

FAILURE OR SUCCESS? OUR LEGACY FROM HENRY ADAMS

Earl N. Harbert

For readers of Henry Adams's *Education*, no single word of that classic text resonates more powerfully than "Failure"—the title of chapter 20. Finally, in the pages of his skillfully contrived self history, this simple declaration comes to serve Adams as a verdict on the lives and works of an entire American generation, including such friends as Clarence King, and even Adams himself. Appearing only a little beyond halfway through the book, the authorial label of "failure" strikes first-time readers as premature, arbitrary, and most of all, confusing. Nevertheless, diligent undergraduate students complete the remaining two hundred pages of the *Education* before they become bold enough to raise their questions out loud:

"How could Henry Adams call his life a failure?"

"What does he mean by 'failure' anyhow?"

Like Hawthorne's *Scarlet Letter*, Adams's chapter fills a special office.[1] By suggestion and implication, some alternative determination of "success" has tacitly emerged from the entire text, in part because its author has presented that idea with potency enough to complete a mental set of bipolar possibilities—failure and success. Here, the engaged reader has been compelled by Adams the writer to respond—to agree or disagree with the literal text—as a matter of individual judgment, which depends upon a singular evaluation of *all* the evidence. Yet the undergraduate seldom finds much to evaluate.

For more experienced readers of Adams, such evidence grows and multiplies, as each reader becomes familiar with the writer and his history by applying a longer time horizon, extending from the date of Adams's composition and publication, beyond the end of Adams's life, until the present time. For us, this

---

[1]For the most complete discussion of Hawthorne's complex symbol, see Sacvan Bercovitch, *The Office of the Scarlet Letter* (Baltimore and London, 1991). For earlier commentary on Adams, see Earl N. Harbert, "Henry Adams," in *Fifteen American Authors Before 1900* (Madison, Wis., 1984).

lengthening evaluation represents one of the many tasks as-
signed to contemporary criticism. We can expect, by using some
more comprehensive sampling of the record—of the already
well-documented response to Henry Adams, including his person, writings, and relationship with the world—to extend an existing line of general human interest, and perhaps even to find
evidence sufficient for determining the failure or success of his
legacy, at least to our own satisfaction. With that end in view, our
investigation now commences.

As always with Adams, the chief danger that we face is oversimplification. In part, this situation is both inevitable and encour-
aging, because the flow of new information about Henry Adams
remains continuous—and much of what is recent must be regarded as important to every reader of Adams. In short, then, the
vitality of Adams as a subject for research and commentary demonstrates one form of his success, even while it serves to inhibit
authoritative judgments. Already it seems clear, for example, that
certain of Henry Adams's letters (such as those to Elizabeth Cameron) rank among the best ever written in English. In general,
these letters display qualities far more artful than any required for
basic communication. Yet as a matter for historical determination,
reputation as a letter-writer—like reputation of other kinds—depends for Adams (or anyone else) on the degree of popular appreciation for the letter as a literary form. So Henry Adams's
success as a letter-writer, like the career of Clarence King as described in chapter 20 of the *Education*, must finally rest on what
Adams calls "ordinary luck"—in this case, the luck of a cultural
marketplace that Adams could neither predetermine nor predict.

In many ways, Adams's luck has so far been extraordinary, certainly better than King's. Almost from the beginning, readers
have been willing to look beyond any merely literal message in
Adams's writing, and to presume the existence of alternative
meanings, usually defined by the reader alone. Thus we confront
such a response as these words of the famous German historian
Hermann von Holst, who inscribed this dedication in a volume
of his own history, a book that has survived as a part of Adams's
personal library:

Henry Adams, Esq. with the highest regards of the author who would
not have made it the main task of his life as a scholar to study the United
States if he considered them "a failure." [2]

---

[2]This inscribed volume is included in the Henry Adams collection at the Massachusetts
Historical Society, Boston, Mass.

Clearly von Holst refused to accept Adams's judgment.

In addition to von Holst, the emerging record shows that other readers have also remained unconvinced by Adams's rhetoric. Indeed, von Holst's response set a pattern for many skeptics who followed, few of whom could have known of the German's dedication to Adams. On the basis of all available evidence then, it seems safe to conclude that Henry Adams's literary method resulted in some overt or covert invitation to read well *beyond* his words, to answer the question that he so often posed for his readers, and finally to search out implications and extensions of Adams's statements. As a whole, his message offered a far-sighted challenge to the reader's understanding and judgment. That challenge has not yet been exhausted.

Even when Adams's apparent subject was the distant past, he wrote so that his message would evolve to fit the future. Not surprisingly, Adams has proved in many ways to be far more modern than he could have anticipated. Today, he remains "relevant," and with regard to his special reputation as a futurist, "ordinary luck" has served Adams well. Yet, despite this continuing relevance, too much of this story of Adams's pervasive influence remains unspoken and largely out of sight to the reader who searches for literal meaning. In her important book, *The Lady and the Virgin: Image, Attitude, and Experience in Twelfth-Century France,* for example, Penny Shine Gold argues the case for historical re-definition with this declaration of need:

We have been told repeatedly, with a uniformity that comes from uncritical acceptance, that the twelfth-century creation of the images of the lady in love literature and of the Virgin Mary indicates a dramatic improvement in attitudes toward women or in the actual position of women in society. Yet few works have actually explored in detail the cultural interrelationships implied in this judgment.[3]

At this point in her "preface," Gold inserts a footnote acknowledgment to Henry Adams's *Mont-Saint-Michel and Chartres,* a book that (in her words) "is the major exception." She continues: "This book is also probably the source, direct or indirect, of many twentieth-century historians' notions of twelfth-century women."[4] Nowhere else in Gold's text or notes is *Chartres* mentioned, although we have been assured of its pathmark critical

---

[3](Chicago, 1985): "Preface," xv.
[4]Ibid.

value. Yet Adams's seminal volume must have played a key role in the formative stages of Gold's thinking, during the decade and more in which her scholarly investigation of the twelfth century was underway, first as a dissertation project and then in preparation for her published book. As that book now appears, however, any larger recognition of Henry Adams's influence remains unwritten in her pages, and Gold's readers are left to infer what they will.

Perhaps Adams's literary technique of indirection has simply proved contagious. Certainly non-literal meaning does represent one important part of his message and legacy; therefore, his example should be expected to have cast a long shadow. In a contrasting way, since the original novelty of Adams's early and enthusiastic endorsement of using primary documents as the necessary foundation for acceptable history has largely faded over time, these opinions of his now seem merely commonplace, in our age of student casebooks. Yet even with this bad "luck," some more specific acknowledgment of Adams's key role as a documentary pioneer lurks in the dark subtext of a recent announcement of forthcoming publication of the papers of Albert Gallatin, President Jefferson's secretary of the treasury, and a much-admired biographical subject of the young Henry Adams. This notice appeared in *Documentary Editing*; in it, the name of Henry Adams, Gallatin's first editor and biographer, does not appear.[5] Surely we agree that what Adams began is worth continuing, although I must confess to having mixed feelings when I read that Adams's original role as Gallatin's single editor will now be filled by an editorial board of ten well-qualified persons, supported by an "advisory board" of thirteen members, headed by another former secretary of the treasury. Somewhere the shade of Henry Adams must be laughing at the results of historical change.

Still, in a substantial way the Gallatin Papers project may be expected to focus welcome attention on Adams's editorial and biographical legacy. More Gallatin volumes—when they appear—should help us to understand Adams's hero in a larger way, and also increase our appreciation for Adams's role in shaping the Gallatin we know today. Briefly, the Gallatin Papers can be expected to alter significantly our present view of Adams's editorial, biographical, and historical methods, while making Albert Gallatin a larger figure in the whole of American history. To

---

[5]September 1988 issue, 28.

judge from the printed words of Adams and others, Gallatin deserves no less. So this extension of vital historical interest prom-
ises real value.

At the same time, however, the general historical process of
gradually enlarging our range of considerations should not be
permitted to cancel out earlier achievements—such as Henry Adams's century-old work on Gallatin or Adams's contributions to
the theory and practice of history. Here, Adams deserves to hold
an influential place. Already we have noted one acknowledgment of debt to him (however understated) written into an important recent contribution to the emerging field of feminist
history. In other contexts as well, we find evidence that contemporary advocates of large-scale historiography often prefer to
make their cases by relying heavily on ideas that earlier found expression in the historical writings of Henry Adams. To cite only a
single example, Arthur M. Schlesinger, Jr., in *The Cycles of American History*, proposes his cyclical theory after candidly admitting
in his foreword: "No one knew the risks of history better than
Henry Adams, whose name is invoked more than once in the
pages that follow."[6] As a presence in contemporary historiography, then, Adams retains both vitality and significance. Certainly
he has endured (if not always prevailed), and at some moments
he emerges as *the* ranking authority from the past.

Here, as a more specialized example, I turn to a recent experiment in historical method, *Thinking in Time: The Uses of History for
Decision-Makers*, written by Richard Neustadt and Ernest May. As
their title suggests, the authors are chiefly interested in applied
history—in how history can be used (rather than misused) in
reaching wise decisions. Briefly, the "decision-makers" of the title emerge as primarily (but not exclusively) high government of-
ficials charged with the responsibility for making sound public
policy, such as national foreign policy. Thus, the practical setting
for these case studies is familiar to many institutional historians;
moreover, that setting would have seemed familiar and even con-
ventional to Henry Adams if the book had appeared one hundred
years earlier.

While writing up their cases, Neustadt and May found need to
mention Henry Adams only once: recommending his *History* to
their own readership of "decision-makers," the authors declare:

Henry Adams's *History of the United States During the Administrations of
Thomas Jefferson and James Madison* reflects not only his feeling that the

---

[6](Boston, 1986), iv.

White House belonged to his family but also intimacy with real politicians of his own time. Although nine volumes long, it is such lively
reading that it seems too short.[7]

Without arguing over the literal truth of the quotation, readers
may yet be puzzled about the specific grounds of Adams's value
for "decision-makers." Nevertheless, some indebtedness of this
book to Henry Adams must be allowed, since the "method" advocated by Neustadt and May echoes Adams's earlier attempts
to analyze representative American political minds in operation.
In fact Henry Adams used the pages of his *History* to show how
political men employed the historical past in the process of
making decisions and taking actions. *Thinking in Time*, while declaring itself to be a pioneering venture in applied history, must
be regarded also as a sympathetic extension into the present of
what Henry Adams had attempted earlier in his most ambitious
historical studies. And now, a hundred years later, in our developing practice of using relevant history to meet some specific
need (whether consciously, as in the method recommended to
decision-makers by Neustadt and May, or unconsciously, as a
matter of psychological investigation) Adams's seminal influence
deserves acknowledgment. For the American reader especially,
every consideration of applied history should bring the ideas of
Henry Adams to mind.

• • • • •

Yet even a wide review of cultural transmissions, will leave
some relatively unexamined, due in part to a lack of adequate information and as often to a lack of space. Here, for example, we
shall not speculate about the impact of Henry Adams's appearance on public television's *Adams Chronicles*, or about his complex
characterization in twentieth-century fiction. At the very least,
however, it should be noted that such timely exposure works to
keep his name alive.

To affirm his *intellectual* presence, on the other hand, requires
some greater demonstration of cultural influence or force. In their
own modest way, of course, the brief acknowledgments that we
have already located in the work of living historians may be regarded as at least a minimal proof of Adams's currency. With this
encouragement, we are ready to survey the cultural field in a

---

[7]*Thinking in Time: The Uses of History for Decision-Makers* (New York, 1986), 266.

more systematic way. First, we note that, as a subject of biographical interest, Henry Adams continues to fascinate, and that no end to this appeal is yet in sight. Instead, new efforts to see the man whole, including both his personal relationships and his authorial (and editorial) achievements, continue.

At the present time, however, Adams is known to the public more as an author than as a personality; he receives nominal credit for a variety and range of published writings, and new attributions seem to be proposed every year. Of course, this literary reputation can be expected to suffer a *not* unmixed fate: On the one hand, at least some fragments of Adams's work seem to be safely canonized—such as that best known chapter (25) of the *Education* ("The Dynamo and the Virgin"), which appears in almost every reputable anthology of American literature. In this situation some kind of reputation seems assured, even though readers of such anthologies may never become informed about any more of Adams's writings. On the other hand, contemporary prospects for Henry Adams's reputation as a letter-writer seem more doubtful, due to circumstances beyond authorial control. Whether the blame is ascribed to historical cause or attributed to bad luck, the situation smacks of irony: for at the same time that the first authoritative edition of Adams's letters finally emerges from the press, the literary genre of the letter appears to have experienced a sharp decline in both popularity and literary importance. In fact, the letter has become a victim of multiple technological displacement, first by the telephone and lately by electronic "messaging." For most readers, and even for many scholars, the letter form has now been reduced to the mundane status of documentary evidence. Ironically, in this process and through no fault of his own, Adams as letter-writer has suffered from "un-ordinary luck" of the same kind that defeated Clarence King.

Turning to Adams the biographer, for his present reputation we need make no such special pleading. As the standard bibliographies testify, in this capacity our author has so far survived the caprice of time. Yet, like the role of the personal letter in human communications, modern biography, in both theory and practice, has moved far beyond every contribution made by Henry Adams, becoming in the process much wider in variations and deeper in acceptable detail. On the subject of Thomas Jefferson, the largest single biographical study contained in Adams's nine-volume *History*, for example, recent years have introduced both the controversial revelations, based on psychological analysis, proposed by Fawn Brodie, and the magisterial portrayal in Dumas Malone's six-volume biography. In contrast to these more recent studies of Jefferson, Henry Adams's portrait now appears pale and unfinished. Yet the fact remains that Adams left behind in his writings many important touchstones for our present understanding, and not only of Jefferson but also of Albert Gallatin, John Randolph, James Madison, John Hay, Clarence King, and key members of the Adams family, among others. In sum, then, Adams's biographical writings have functioned over time to help define the mainstream of scholarly biographical practice, and not surprisingly, present-day biographers have generously acknowledged an indebtedness to him—even when they differ sharply with his interpretations.

Since Adams wrote, however, no portion of the literary marketplace has altered more than that for written lives. Today, we find ourselves inundated by the sea of *un*-scholarly biographies, written (or ghost-written) about still-living business tycoons, rock stars, and cult heroes—often as a part of the public relations effort to promote some media event or even the sale of a product such as automobiles. Again, the current state of biographical writing is much too large a matter for adequate consideration here; but as a sign of the times, this headline from *The Boston Globe* provides a convenient summary: "PEEPSHOW BIOGRAPHIES ARE DENIGRATING THE GENRE."[8] As that bold announcement makes clear, the foundations of popular acceptance have shifted, leaving Henry Adams behind. But not because Adams refused to entertain new biographical ideas.

In particular, I believe that Adams would have readily welcomed personal interviews and oral history as an important complement to written documents and letters. Imagining Adams's opinions concerning our current varieties of popular written biography, on the other hand, leads me to suggest that he might well discern in recent cultural history the operation of "Gresham's Law of Biography." Surely, the sensational has largely replaced the demonstrable. In any case, here the vital presence of Adams's influence remains purely intellectual. It is a matter of conjecture, yet for me, nonetheless real.

Certainly, great literary popularity may still be expected to generate wide imitation, and *The Education of Henry Adams* has proven to be no exception. Autobiographical—more or less—in authorial intention, this now-classic piece of best-selling Americana showcases an intimidating complexity of method, structure, and

---

[8]23 October 1988.

message. Together, these characteristics have guaranteed the book a place in the still-vital confessional tradition of self-examination. In fact, imitators continue to surface everywhere, but especially in the United States, where education is pursued with missionary zeal. Yet no later American has been able to capture more than a taste of Adams's book—often merely an echo of his tone or title. Here, only a comprehensive survey of these echoes—calibrated against the groundswell of popular interest in autobiographical and confessional forms, a trend that marks this age as one of "every man (woman) his (her) autobiographer"—would usefully determine the exact influence of Adams's most read volume. For our purposes, however, a few examples will serve. Let's begin by recalling the unusual circumstances surrounding the original private printing and the later commercial publication of Adams's *Education*. In effect, that book may be considered to have filled a dual role of influence, first on the private and then on the larger public audience of readers. Searching for a modern parallel, we encounter what may be the most remarkable of recent American confessionals in *The Inman Diary: A Public and Private Confession*, first published (in an abridged edition) in 1985.[9]

Its author, Arthur Inman, unlike Adams, set out to make this one book the single sustained literary work of his entire life. Accordingly, Inman composed a gigantic diary with the intention of having it published after his death, and he made arrangements (including financial ones) to guarantee that result. Even in an abridged form, the *Diary* offers its reader a remarkably open window into Inman's reclusive life. However, the complexity of the author's method also guarantees that any future biographer, if there is to be one, will be confronted by a complex set of problems.

Here, with more modest purpose in view than that of the biographer, we can use the Inman *Diary* as a fascinating, if entirely unofficial, public record of the author's times, including his responses to the literature he read and re-read. With Henry Adams in mind, we turn to Inman's entry for 11 September 1933:

Some critics consider *The Education of Henry Adams* to be one of the finest books in American literature. I have striven without success to read it. Adams is vain, acrid of wit, pessimistic. His pages are sequined with notable characters, yet few are notably drawn. His is a vainglorious mind, flashy, pompous, purposely inhuman. He certainly does deem Henry Adams a smart fellow. . . .

---

[9]This was edited by Daniel Aaron (Cambridge, Mass., 1985).

If there was warmth in Adams, he hid it very well. I dislike the man, dislike his books and letters.[10]

Inman's dismissal seems convincing, yet he had not finished with Adams or the *Education*. Without explanation, the diarist picks up the theme again on 26 September 1943:

The further I progress into *The Education of Henry Adams*, the more I dislike it. It is a stupid book. The author's bland self-conceit is boring. The author must have been an empty portfolio of a man with only the crest and record of his family to give him the appearance of prestige. I find myself for the time unable to finish the book. What Yeats said of Shakespeare, that he is "only a mass of magnificent fragments" is true in reverse of Adams: He is only a mass of wearisome fragments.[11]

Just what drove Inman back to the *Education* remains uncertain, and nowhere is there evidence to show that the diarist ever reached chapter 20 of the *Education,* to read of "Failure." What does seem clear is that Adams simply failed to establish any rapport with reader Inman. But even so, the *Education* as a total message did *not* fail to exact from this reader a notable response— both visceral and intellectual.

Today, we benefit by reading *both* Adams and Inman. Thus, we can extend (and further complicate) this single line of historical interest by measuring Inman's critical response to Adams against the larger record of all the diarist's literary opinions, expressed throughout the *Diary* (and, in theory at least, expanded to include those expressed in portions that remain unpublished). On just such a basis, we may wish to label Inman an unperceptive reader.

• • • • •

So far, of course, every answer to the larger question of Adams's success or failure seems merely tentative and largely subjective. The evidence, closely studied, becomes ambiguous and unreliable. In place of conviction, we offer only ambition; so in frustration we turn to a comparativist approach. In contrast to Inman's response, another line of interest cast by Adams and the *Education* leads in a different direction, to the famous art historian Bernard Berenson. In fact, the Adams-Berenson relationship offers an especially noteworthy case of historical influence because

---

[10]Ibid., 2: 868.
[11]Ibid., 2: 1187.

it has been studied closely at both ends by the same scholar, Ernest Samuels, the meticulous biographer of both men. Samuels considers their personal relationship at length, and concludes that Berenson knew Adams as a personal friend and conversationalist, as well as an established author, who had written letters and books much discussed among members of the Berenson circle. Since the friendship ripened quickly after their first meeting in 1903, Berenson was able to read both *Mont-Saint-Michel and Chartres* and *The Education of Henry Adams* as a privileged member of the select audience for Adams's private printings of fewer than one hundred copies.

On the surface, of course, it will seem obvious that Berenson and Adams must have shared an interest in architecture and art, and that we might expect *Chartres* to have registered a powerful influence on the thinking of the younger Berenson. Guided by Samuels's thoughtful summation in the pages of his *Henry Adams*, we willingly accept some definition of their friendship based on common interest but also affected by quite different personalities:

Berenson shared Adams's passion for the Gothic cathedrals, as he too was a belated Pre-Raphaelite. The affinity ran deep, and the tie endured almost to the end of Adams's life. Adams acknowledged that in a world of "dismal flatirons" Berenson was the only one of his acquaintances "who bites hard enough to smart."[12]

These words of the dual biographer define a personal "affinity" that deserves to be acknowledged even though we shall not explore it here.

Instead, we turn away from *Chartres*, and from architecture and art, to study the less obvious evidence of influence on Berenson that derives from Adams's *Education* and letters. Now, the common theme becomes more personal and less celebratory, an expression of loss and regret; and we find it expressed in Berenson's writings.

Ernest Samuels has noted Berenson's anguished expressions of loss and regret at the time of Adams's death (1918), as well as the art historian's declarations made during the 1950s, that he considered himself to be a "disciple" of Adams. In private, Berenson began to demonstrate some form of kinship with Adams as early as 1929, when the art historian reenacted Adams's favorite role, that of retrospective author. Berenson first revised and then com-

---

[12]*Henry Adams* (Cambridge, Mass., 1989), 362.

bined his four modest studies of individual artists into his renowned classic, *The Italian Painters of the Renaissance*, published in 1930. This occasion made Berenson into a reviser-editor of his own writings; also it led him to review his earlier career while he worked. As a result, the outwardly confident art authority relied on a private letter to reveal deep misgivings about himself: "The man who wrote these little volumes . . . should not have let himself be led astray into picture fancying and expertising. He should have gone on to write the aesthetics and history of all humanistic art. That and that alone would have meant success."[13] In Berenson's case (as in Adams's before) seeds of personal doubt and failure had taken deep root and they were not to be denied, at least in private. Once again, Samuels's understanding proves useful to us, when he notes that, henceforth, expressions of regret will provide an insistent refrain in Berenson's private correspondence.

By 1940, Berenson had begun to bring his own doubts into public view, as he prepared the documentary self-analysis that Samuels calls a "semiautobiographical" manuscript, which was published in 1949 as *Sketch for a Self-Portrait*. In the pages of that printed volume, the pervasive influence of Henry Adams's *Education* can be easily traced. In fact, this vital connection between two famous authors has elsewhere been described with admirable exactness by their common biographer, who explains the transmission in these terms:

Adams . . . had tried to define his role in the world and to explain why, though apparently successful, his career had seemed to him a failure. That theme of failure struck a responsive chord in Berenson, and as he put down his reminiscences and reflections from day to day he tried to answer the question of why . . . he had lost his way. Who and what was he really, he seemed to ask himself. All the egocentric concerns which had colored his letters, all the intense self-contemplation which had marked his progress through life, came to the surface now for critical inspection.[14]

Relying on both sensitive appreciation and broad knowledge, Samuels draws an indelible line of influence from Adams to Berenson, and goes ahead to detail why their common "spiritual loss was great." For Samuels's readers, the entire chronology demonstrates a process of continuing intellectual influence: In brief outline, publishing in 1989 and 1987, Samuels looks back to

---

[13]*Bernard Berenson: The Making of a Legend* (Cambridge, Mass., 1987), 377.
[14]Ibid., 466-467.

Berenson writing in the 1940s and 1950s, to trace the impact of Adams's statements of 1904 and shortly after.

With this modest act of informed scholarship, then, the contemporary scholar has established both a human and a literary connection; he has placed the two writers and their messages along a single thematic path, one that Samuels finds cause to label "unabashed introspection." Much earlier, composing pages of his *Education* long before Berenson could read them, Adams also felt compelled to trace the origins of his own exercise in self-analysis back to the example of St. Augustine. So, as the line of influence grows longer, we gain in incremental understanding, and for us as readers, some feeling of success or satisfaction becomes accessible.

Of course not every reader can plot a fix along every one of Adams's various lines of interest. Still, from Adams's life and works, many ideas continue to emerge and radiate, and to function together as a multiplicity of invitations to read and understand. Of their continuing power to fascinate, there can be no guarantee, as Adams well understood. But at the present time, more than one hundred and fifty years after his birth, the historical record speaks eloquently of Henry Adams's success in creating dialogue.

INDEX OF NAMES